MU TAU
PANKRATION

VOLUME I/CONCEPTS AND SKILLS OF "ALL-POWERS" COMBAT

by Grandmaster Jim Arvanitis

Copyright ©1997 by Jim Arvanitis
Second Edition
All rights reserved under International and
Pan-American Copyright Conventions.
World rights reserved, including the right
of translation.
Published in the United States by Spartan
Publications, a division of Spartan Martial
Arts Enterprises, Inc.
No part of the contents of this book may be
reproduced without the written permission
of the publishers.
ISBN: 0-9657442-0-5
Library of Congress Catalog Number: 804-046

DISCLAIMER: Neither the author or the publisher assumes any responsibility for the use or misuse of information contained in this book.

Spartan Publications

BOSTON, MASSACHUSETTS

DEDICATION

To my wonderful wife and sons for their support and encouragement throughout the years, and to my Greek ancestors for developing the roots of this fascinating martial art.

ACKNOWLEDGMENTS

Participants:

Front Row (from left):   **Nick Hines, Jim Hines.**
Back Row (from left):   **Mark Nash**, **Eric Hill**.

Photographs by **Chrys Gardner, Katherine Ayoob, Richard Balboni,** and **David Lowden**.

Graphics by **Bryson Arvanitis**.

All illustrations by Jim Arvanitis.

CONTENTS

    ♦ Mu Tau Pankration Terminology
    ♦ Mu Tau Pankration Rankings
    ♦ MTP Attributes
    ♦ MTP Products

GRANDMASTER JIM ARVANITIS BIOGRAPHY

Grandmaster **Jim Arvanitis** is internationally renowned as the "father" of modern pankration. He took up the study of Hellenic boxing and wrestling at an early age, and soonthereafter learned of the fighting style of his ancestors called *pankration*. A driven athlete with strong ethnic ties, Jim made it his life's work to rebuild the ancient "all-powers" combative form into a modern "cross-training" martial arts system.

To expand upon his unarmed combat skills, especially in the area of standup striking, Arvanitis studied a number of other martial arts styles including muay-Thai (Thai boxing) under former bantamweight champion Supaachai Nittiyiapatinaii and French Savate with Canadian savateur Bernard LaChance. He also worked extensively with established practitioners of combat judo. The Greek-American is an avid reader and analyzed a number of other fighting methods. After years of research, Jim developed the first contemporary style of pankration which he named *mu tau*. A unique composite of his previous studies, Arvanitis' system integrated modern techniques with principles modeled after those of his ancient forebears. It was Arvanitis who revived the almost-extinct art, introduced it to the United States as early as 1971, and popularized it throughout the world in the years that followed.

Along with his almost fanatical obsession with training, Arvanitis is a highly-respected historian, technician, and innovator of the Greek martial arts. As a competitor, he had outstanding records in boxing and wrestling. Jim was also a seasoned street-fighter during his earlier years, and was undefeated in impromtu challenge matches. The mu tau founder has been featured in all of the top martial arts magazines, including *Inside Kung-Fu, Official Karate, Fighting Champions, Karate Illustrated, Martial Arts Masters, Jiu-Jitsu Grappling Guide, Inside Karate, Fighting Stars, American Karate, Martial Arts Ultimate Warriors, World of Martial* Arts and *Karate International*. He has also been on the cover of *Black Belt*. The master pankratiast has made numerous television appearances, conducted seminars throughout the United States, Canada, and Europe, and is listed in the *Martial Arts Encyclopedia, Who's Who in American Martial Arts*, and *Martial Arts Founders & Masters* for his many accomplishments. Arvanitis also authored a previous book

*As featured on the cover of **Black Belt** (1973).

on his art in 1980. His film credits include starring in an introductory video series available from *Panther Productions*, considered the world leader in martial arts action tapes. Other physical feats include his now famous world record for the "thumb pushup", using both arms and but one arm. Arvanitis is among the first to have been bestowed the title of grandmaster of the Hellenic martial arts and has received numerous Hall of Fame induction awards. He is a member of the prestigious *World Head of Family Sokeship Council*.

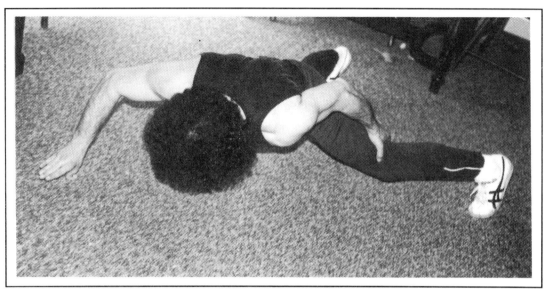

The single-arm thumb pushup.

Among Arvanitis' students have been law enforcement personnel, bodyguards, and members of the military's elite special forces. Arvanitis was instrumental in preparing many Army soldiers stationed at Fort Devens in Ayer, Massachusetts for the Persian Gulf conflict in the late 1980s.

Today, Jim Arvanitis exemplifies the classic Spartan athlete by training religiously, running at least ten miles daily, working out with weights three to four days per week, and keeping his skills sharp by hitting equipment and sparring with his top followers. His teaching prowess is in great demand at seminars throughout the world. The innovative martial artist has combined natural athletic ability with a diligent work ethic to become the most famous practitioner of Greek descent in the Twentieth century. His efforts alone have been instrumental in reviving an ancient Greek legacy, one which is believed to be the oldest form of all-out, utilitarian combat on record.

INTRODUCTION

The martial arts are as old as man himself. For every country on earth, a unique form of fighting has been created which is indigenous to that particular culture. Greek pankration is among the oldest of these, having been well-documented before the coming of Christ, and having been practiced for both sport and military purposes. An original part of the earliest Olympic games, pankration has influenced modern martial arts throughout the world to a degree that few of today's practitioners are aware of. The currently popular UFC (Ultimate Fighting Championships) and other similar combative events are closely patterned after the ancient Greek sport of no-holds-barred combat. Even the newer Japanese styles of shootfighting and pancrase profess to be pankration derivatives.

Since my first book went out of print in 1986, I have received hundreds of requests to release a new text. Since that time, the Greek fighting art that I have worked many years to revive and remodel has continued to evolve into its present form. This work, then, is to serve not so much as a "how-to" manual on learning pankration techniques, but to provide the martial arts enthusiast with an overall look at what this Greek art once was and what it is today. While there have been excellent accounts of Greece's combat sports in prior works, none can be considered a complete treatment of pankration. It is the objective of this book to educate the martial arts community about this essential component of systematized combat, one that is sometimes overlooked or even forgotten.

In truth, the original pankration is no longer with us. Due to a number of factors, it died out thousands of years ago. Today, the term "pankration" is often used as a conceptual label for integrating striking and grappling techniques, or what has become more popularly known as martial arts "cross-training." Although it was formerly the name for a competitive event, pankration has become an eclectic style composed of modern skills and training methodology, while, at the same time, perpetuating an ancient legacy, one rich in history, myth, and tradition. However, modern proponents of Greek heritage will place the practice of the art form before that of the sport, carefully observing the philosophical ideals that are the backbone of any martial discipline. Lacking such standards will only contribute to its demise, as was the case with Greece's early creation.

My first contact with pankration occurred while studying Greco-Roman wrestling and boxing as a teenager in Greece. Although my original purpose in this undertaking was to learn personal defense, it eventually became secondary to bringing recognition to my Spartan forebears for their achievement. Thus, the primary mission was to eventually redesign and somehow rebuild the ancient sport into an art from what little remained. For me, Greece's contribution to the pool of martial arts knowledge was immense and was not to be ignored.

My next objective was to reshape Greek combat into an effective, practical means of self-protection geared more for the street rather than tournaments. I found that many of the conventional styles during this era (i.e. karate and kung-fu) were more concerned with ritual and preset forms rather than realism, something the Greeks had long advocated in their native combative sports. Another goal in this restructuring process was to provide a vehicle for athletic discipline, complete with training methods that would enable me and those who followed a means of maintaining excellent fitness and nutritional habits throughout our lifetimes. I believe that a martial artist is not one possessing magical powers, but is primarily an athlete and must be in top shape at all times. It offended me to see high-ranking "masters" who were overweight with a protruding waistline and in poor condition.

Needless to say, this became a lifelong commitment. History, concepts, and technique, in that order, became my guide or "blueprint" in this process. As I had discovered from other Greek martial artists knowledgeable in the "old ways", most of today's Western and Asian combat styles contained techniques that indirectly were derived from pankration through the passing of time. In fact, most of the modern hand techniques used in Western boxing and the Oriental martial arts can be found in the archaeological record of vases, wall paintings, and sculpted statues left behind by the ancient Greeks. Thus, in studying a diversity of techniques, both of Greek influence and of other styles, I attempted to fill the void that was left by the antiquated art.

Obviously, I would have been unable to bring pankration to this next level, if you will, without the many historical resources and the willingness of those experts of Greek lineage to share their wisdom with me. To them, I owe a great deal of gratitude for supporting my endeavor.

In the early part of the 1970s when pankration was first exposed to the American martial arts scene, it received outcries of criticism from the "classical establishment." These individuals, bound by their devotion to the more accepted styles of karate, taekwondo, and kung-fu, condemned pankration as a "savage, barbaric practice." Perhaps, their arrogance and lack of comprehension served to cloud their vision of where the martial arts would be headed in the 90s. Today, of course, thanks in part to the Brazilian influence, the effectiveness of purely upright combat systems is in question. In no-holds-barred combative contests, grapplers and ground technicians have proven over and over that they are able to take down and completely dominate what was once considered the invincible way to fight. Surprisingly, this is nothing new to the pankratiast, for his ancestors have been practicing a similar approach to combat for thousands of years before this.

With the current interest in ground combat and hybrid fighting, there are many individuals alleging to be practicing pankration. While there are certainly many qualified exponents of Greek descent now openly teaching variations of it both in Greece and in the United States, there are also those who are merely using the name to conveniently represent their amalgam of techniques. What is interesting to note is that prior to my introduction of pankration's history and concepts in America, there were few, if any, martial artists even remotely familiar with it. Pankration meant nothing more to them than some exotic European pastry. And while one need not be of Greek blood to be a bonafide pankratiast, it is highly unlikely that many of these claimants have studied the true art. Their limited knowledge has undoubtedly been obtained through the countless magazine articles that have featured pankration and myself over the past two decades.

Sadly enough, this is not unusual conduct in the martial arts. It is justifiable for some to adopt the current buzzword, dream up an impressive but unsubstantiated background, and then ride on the publicity that has been conveniently established before them. This is the case with many of the new crop of so-called "American pankratiasts." Yet regardless of their ramblings and arguments in defense of their claims, the indisputable fact remains that prior to 1973, few had even heard of pankration and I was the first to make it known in many parts of the world. Even in its native homeland, pankration did not reappear until 1986. These statements are not purely of unwarranted arrogance, but are supported by continued accomplishment which is fully documented.

Naturally, change is essential in the growth and improvement of any art. Although the roots and basic framework remain intact, the skills of the system will adjust according to kineseological developments which are reflective of our cultural advancements. On the technical side, pankration is a mixture of boxing and wrestling that includes kicking and submission holds. Its modern descendent has many aspects in common with Japanese and Brazilian jiujitsu styles, as well as with Thai kickboxing (muay Thai) and even combat judo. What is important to note here is that martial arts, technically, are more alike than different. The major dissimilarities are in strategy; that is, whether a style is oriented to waging combat from an upright position or on the ground, or whether it favors grappling or striking.

In mu tau pankration, or **MTP** for short, a student is offered the best of both worlds, and is prepared to defend himself in any possible situation, be it against one adversary or many, or in either an unarmed or armed conflict. Much depends on the individual's body type as well as the physical build and reactions of his opponent. For example, it would never be prudent to exchange blows with a better boxer than you. In this case, it might be a wiser choice to go to the ground and grapple. But in a situation where you are facing two or more attackers, it would be more reasonable to stay on your feet and utilize striking skills. These are not radical new ways of thinking about combat, just common sense.

While there are currently a small, but growing, number of palaestrae (training facilities) in the United States and Canada, there are reportedly thousands of active practitioners throughout Europe. Greece, France, and Spain each have their own government-backed organizations, and are conducting contests regularly. When Athens became the host site for the 2004 Olympics, pankration was entered as a "demo" sport. It is now the goal to begin preparing competitors for this special event, one which preserves the tradition of the very first Games. Obviously, there is much work to do in the coming years to make this dream a reality.

As the art continues to grow, one should expect to see many versions of pankration in practice. Some will be more stylized with an emphasis on forms, this being the influence of many Greek martial artists making the transition from traditional karate. The other approach is more reality-based with the focus on optimal self-defense skills and pragmatic training. This style appeals to a special brand of athlete and not just anyone.

This is the first volume of a planned series on the mu tau pankration system. It focuses on its history, basic upright and groundfighting skills, modern training methods, and an introduction to combat strategy. The next volume will emphasize tactical applications based on the elements found in this book.

Although it has been used as a model for some recently-emerging martial arts styles around the globe, one must not lose sight of the fact that pankration is a product of the Western world. It is NOT an Asian development, be it Japanese, Chinese, Korean, etc. Pankration comes from Greece. Indeed, the art has a long and proven history. From its legends that rival the mythology of the gods to its adaptations for today's streets, the all-powers combat system of the Greeks has come full circle into the Twentieth Century. My ambition in writing this book is to provide insight into this very significant link in martial arts evolution.

Jim Arvanitis

I/HISTORY OF GREEK MARTIAL ARTS

The Greek race is well-known for its many achievements in the Pre-Christian era. Along with literature, science, and philosophy, their military and athletic developments are without equal. Credit belongs to them for both the word "athlete" and the ideal it expresses. It is also the Greek soldier who would represent the standard for the rest of the world to follow for centuries. It was during Greece's Classical age (seventh - fourth century BC) that athletics and the fighting arts, in particular, would make its mark in Greek history and in ancient Western civilization.

There were several reasons for the popularity of Grecian combat during this time. The most important of these was the need of the city states, or *polis*, to prepare its citizens for warfare. Second was the worship of health, beauty, and strength - the real religion of the Greeks. The ancient Greeks were as health conscious as many Americans are today. Last but not least was the characteristic Greek love for competition and victory, which highly-trained athletes aspired to in the athletic festivals of the ancient world. These included the games at Olympia and Delphi (Pythian festival), Corinth (Isthmian festival), Nemea, and other pan-Hellenic events. A man who won at all four festivals received the special title of *periodonikes*. The classic Greek athlete was akin to today's modern martial artist who practices his chosen style for purposes of personal defense, health, and self-expression.

Although many countries claim responsibility for the origin of the martial arts, ancient Greece has the best historical records substantiating their developments. Much of this information comes from old vase paintings and sculptures depicting early Greek warriors competing in combat, as well as direct quotes of famous poets and philosophers. Many historians believe that early unarmed and armed combat techniques entered Greece from Egypt. Greece then modified and refined these techniques, which later found their way into India.

The martial arts practiced by the ancient Greeks were first established for military training. Later, competitions were created to simulate combat. These combat sports date back to the earliest Olympic Games, which commenced in 776 B.C. at Olympia. From this date onward, the Games were staged every four years until A.D. 393. While military training familiarized the Greeks with the fighting arts, the love of competition spurred them on to mastery. The three major combative sports included in the Games were wrestling, boxing, and the deadly pankration. The Greeks referred to these as the "heavy events", since, due to the lack of weight divisions in antiquity, they became the domain of the large and strong. These forms of hand-to-hand fighting are the earliest thoroughly documented martial arts styles, and stand out as the probable forerunners of today's combative disciplines.

GREEK WRESTLING (PALE)

Wrestling is Greece's oldest combat sport, having been introduced into the Olympics of 708 B.C. Wrestling appealed deeply to the ancients and was highly valued as a form of weaponless military training. The poet Pindar claimed that the Olympic Games came into existence as a result of a wrestling match between the gods Zeus and Cronus. Like all classic Greek athletes, the wrestlers wore no clothing, and often oiled themselves to keep dirt out of their pores. Powder was then added to their hands to ensure a good grip.

There were two distinct versions of the sport, differing according to the holds employed and the methods of deciding the victor of a contest. These included:

Kato pale, or ground wrestling, was decided when one competitor acknowledged defeat. This was indicated by raising one's right hand with the index finger pointed.

Orthia pale, or upright-style wrestling, in which the objective was simply to throw the opponent to the ground. Three falls constituted a loss for that fighter, with the winner declared the *triakter*. Some considered the Grecian upright wrestling style to be the most practical unarmed training for war. The *hoplites*, or Greek soldiers, could not afford to get involved in lengthy ground combat during battle, so throwing the enemy to the ground while remaining on their feet seemed the most effective tactical method to many of the early Greek purists.

Ancient Greek wrestling had no time limits and no defined ring or fighting area. It also lacked weight classifications: every contestant entered the tough open division, which placed the smaller man at an extreme disadvantage. The contest consisted of the best out of three falls. A fall was defined as touching the ground with the knees. Once a wrestler threw his opponent, he would pin his foe's shoulders, thereby winning the contest.

Shoulder throw.
Greek vase, circa 500 B.C.

Much of the action allowed leg and shoulder throws, holds, and foot sweeps. Strikes of any kind were illegal. Sacrifice throws, ground fighting, and finishing techniques were well known, but were generally reserved for the pankration or "all-powers" event.

Ancient Greek wrestling favored upright fighting as opposed to ground combat, although there is evidence that some ground wrestling did occur. The wrestlers commenced a bout by seeking control of each other's wrists or neck as a prelude for follow-up offensives. Another means of engagement was the underhook, a hold obtained by grasping underneath the adversary's shoulder in preparation for a throw.

A number of vase paintings show attempts of taking an opponent down by tackling his legs or clinching him about the midsection. One extremely effective technique was the waist lock which was applied from either the front, much like a bearhug, or behind one's foe. Being caught in this hold was a sign of serious disadvantage. It often was followed by a maneuver known as the "heave." Upon defending against a leg takedown, the wrestler gripped his opponent around the back of the waist, hoisted him feet first into the air, and then slammed him down on his head. This might be called a "piledriver" in modernized wrestling.

The "heave", a throwing technique that often followed a reverse waistlock.
Greek bronze, Hellinistic era.

The offensive wrestler applies a reverse waistlock and prepares
to hoist his opponent feet first into the air.
Greek vase, 525-510 B.C.

The great champion Theseus counters
his rival's attack with a waistlock and
prepares to throw him.
Greek vase, 500 B.C.

Wrestlers trained at either of two facilities -- the *palaestra* or the *gymnopaidia* -- both of which were centers for the practice of the fighting arts. Most palaestrae were buildings within the city walls much like large houses. They were owned by private individuals and were equipped with dressing rooms, lounges, and storerooms which contained the oil and powder applied by the wrestlers during practice. Practice was held in the center courtyards, which were normally covered with fine sand. The athletes were first taught basic throwing techniques and maneuvers, which was followed by more sophisticated combinations.

Waistlock from the rear flank which the
defending wrestler is attempting to break
by tearing at the encircling arm.
Greek vase, 360/359 B.C.

Wrestlers struggling on the ground.
Greek vase, 525-510 B.C.

14

A classic match between Theseus and Kerkyon with the former applying a head-lock as Kerkyon attempts to grip the leg. *Greek vase, 510 B.C.*

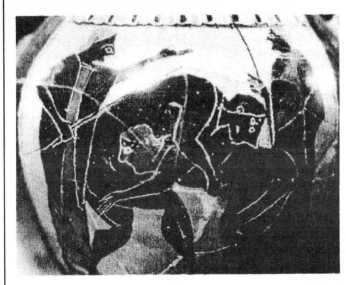

Against a leg tackle, the wrestler on the left sprawls his opponent by gripping him about the waist while dropping his weight forward. *Greek vase, 6th century B.C.*

As a means of physical development, wrestling was designed to teach not only grappling skills but also an aesthetic sense of balance, grace, and finesse. This emphasis on "clean" technique had a definite impact on the manner in which competitive wrestling was conducted as the Greeks sought not only victory but victory with grace and style. Poor technique was unacceptable.

In contrast to the palaestra, the gymnopaidia was under the ownership of the polis and was administered by publicly-appointed officials. All types of athletic endeavors were played in this spacious outdoor sports ground located outside of the city. The gymnopaidia also had wrestling facilities, but served as a center of boxing and pankration training as well. Special trainers were employed to coach citizens and athletes. Training in empty-hand fighting techniques was provided by the *paidotribes* and *gymnastes*, while armed combat was taught by the *hoplomachos* (Greek: weapons specialists), usually to the wealthy.

Theseus counters a leg tackle by Kerkyon by catching him under the arms. He now is in excellent position to either throw his opponent or apply a front headlock.
Greek vase, 460-450 B.C.

The gymnopaidia also served as the training place for the *epheboi*, young men in their latter teens who were required to have two years of intensive military, athletic, and physical education. In addition to unarmed combat and weapons training, the young Spartans learned the *Pyrrhic*, a dance-like exercise where the trainees, armed with shields and javelins, performed different offensive movements and defenses. This form of training was considered so effective that Socrates once remarked that "The best dancer is also the best warrior."

Wrestler on right prepares to throw his opponent by grasping his wrist and underhooking his left arm.
Greek vase, 366 B.C.

The Pyrrhic is included in this passage from the *Laws* by the great philosopher Plato (approximately 427 - 347 B.C.): "The war dance has a different character, and may be properly called the Pyrrhic; it depicts the

16

motions of eluding blows and shots of every kind by various devices of swerving, yielding ground, leaping from the ground or crouching; as well as the contrary motions which lead to a posture of attack, and aim at the reproduction of the shooting of arrows, casting of darts, and dealing in all kinds of blows. In these dances the upright, well-braced posture which represents the good body and good mind, and in which the bodily members are in the main kept straight, is the kind of attitude we pronounce right, that which depicts their contrary, wrong."

The wrestler on the right attempts a hip throw but is foiled by the opponent's tight waistlock.
Greek vase, 520 B.C.

Greek dancing was closely connected with religion, and formed part of all religious festivals and processions. The dance was dramatic and imitative, and exercised every part of the body. Some dances were definitely athletic or military in character. In Sparta, the dancers imitated all movements of wrestling.

Perhaps the most famous and successful of the Olympic wrestling champ-ions was Milon of Kroton. After winning his first Olympic victory in boy's wrestling, he achieved five victories in the men's division. At the age of forty years, he attempted a bid for a sixth title, only to be defeated by a younger man.

The grappler on the left has secured a headlock on his rival, and prepares to throw him over his hip.
Greek vase, 425 B.C.

Wrestling did not rank as a brutal combat sport by the Greeks. Few stories present an image of it as being particularly bloody and violent or having been the cause of numerous fatalities to athletes. These characteristics were more of the boxing and pankration events.

Kato pale or ground wrestling was more reserved for the pankration, although groundwork was frequently employed in ancient Greek wrestling.
Greek vase, 360/359 B.C.

GREEK BOXING (PUGME)

Boxing appears to have been first practiced in the Minoan civilization of Crete around 3000 to 1000 B.C. The fighters wore protective headgear, and there is speculation that kicking comprised an integral part of the art's techniques. One Cretan vase bears testimony to this by showing a fallen fighter kicking upward at his opponent. According to mythology, Apollo invented boxing. He was said to have defeated and killed Phorbas, a boxer who urged travelers through Delphi to compete against him. Philostratus, however, claimed that Greek boxing was pioneered by the Spartans.

Boxing was first introduced into the Olympic Games of 688 B.C. The first victor was Onomastus of Smyrna, who was said to have drawn up the rules for the sport. Like wrestling, boxing bouts had no weight divisions and the action was conducted in an open area rather than a roped-off ring as in today's matches. Blows were allowed with both the fist and the open hand; few punches were prohibited. Surprisingly, there was no rule against striking a downed opponent.

There were also no rounds or time limits with many contests continuing until either contestant was knocked out or raised his right hand as a sign of defeat. Boxing could therefore be a waiting game and a test of stamina. If a long match occurred without the declaration of a clear-cut winner, both fighters could opt for *klimax*. In klimax, an agreement was made to trade blows until one or the other dropped, and neither man would attempt to block or evade the attacks. The story of Creugas and Damoxenus illustrates this type of fighting arrangement. In 400 B.C. at the Nemean Games, these two combatants, one from Syracuse, the other from Epidamnus, struggled into the dusk without a decision. They finally agreed to permit each other to strike one last blow, unresisted, to settle the issue. Creugas struck first, punching Damoxenus solidly in the head. Damoxenus, however, weathered the blow, and ordered his rival to raise his left arm. He then struck Creugas with his open hand, spear-like, with such force that it penetrated Creugas' side, killing him instantly.

As the boxer on the right prepares to deliver an uppercut, his opponent has landed first with an open-hand strike to the face.
Greek vase, 6th century B.C.

The Greek boxer's stance featured a relatively wide spacing of the feet, with the chin down and the hands held high to protect the face. The front hand was normally extended, sometimes opened, and was employed for both defense and attack. The rear hand was used for hooks and uppercuts. Chopping blows to the top of the head, utilizing the bottom of the closed fist, were also popular. The favorite targets for one's blows included the point of the chin, the bridge of the nose, and the sensitive nerve centers surrounding the ears. There is also evidence that blows to the groin were also permitted.

Many boxing technicians were classified as "headhunters", focusing their punches to the head and face although the Greeks were fully aware of the effectiveness of a sustained body attack. The body, being larger and less mobile than the head, was logistically a better target for slowing one's opponent down, thereby opening the head for finishing blows. Evasive footwork and defensive skills were not highly-developed at this time, the fighters relying more on their ability to withstand punishment and dish out more than that of their adversaries. Backing away from blows was considered a sign of cowardice. The victor of a match often emerged bruised and bloodied but in far better shape than his defeated rival.

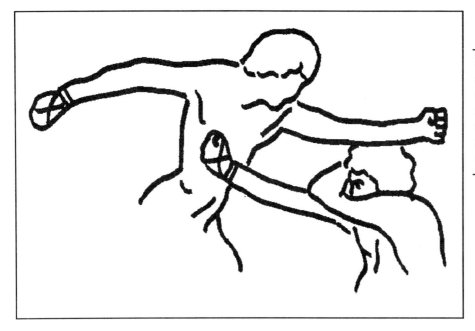

Body punching was not as popular as head shots, but many boxers found the technique effective in taking the fight out of their opponents.

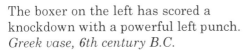

The boxer on the left has scored a knockdown with a powerful left punch. *Greek vase, 6th century B.C.*

The boxers fought barehanded at first, but later wrapped *himantes*, or straps of soft ox-hide around their hands to strengthen their wrists and steady their fingers. Himantes were wrapped around the first knuckles of the fingers, then ran diagonally across the palm onto the back of the hand, leaving the thumb uncovered. Then they were tied around the wrist or forearm. The forms of these hand wraps evolved with straps of harder leather added around the knuckles to make the blows even more devastating.

Alterations to the himantes brought about significant changes in the techniques of the sport. When the thongs were softer, boxing required skill, agility, and good technique with a particular emphasis on offense. The introduction of the sharp thongs slowed the contest, the boxers paying greater attention to defense. Skill gradually became secondary to brute force.

The Roman invention of the *caestus*, a glove weighted with iron and with protruding spikes, transformed Greek boxing into an inhuman and deadly contest. In Rome it was not unusual for such public brutality, as it was the rule rather than the exception, to quench the spectator's thirst for gore and violence. This alteration, however, diminished the skill and aesthetic value that the Greek race had come to admire in their athletes. Rarely, if ever, did a true Greek pugilist participate in the savage gladiatorial arenas of Rome, even though they were often tempted by higher purses and positions within the powerful Roman empire. As such, combat between slaves became more popular than the athletic skills of those who were free.

Left: Ancient Greek boxer wearing the himantes on his fists.
Greek statue, First century B.C.

Below: Roman pugilist wearing the deadly caestus.
Roman bronze statue.

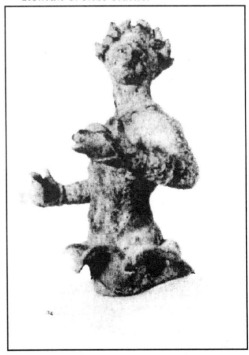

Boxing competition was fierce with the prime objective to hurt one's opponent. There was little evidence of sportsmanship or respect displayed between fighters, with no traditional handshake before the bout and hug afterward. Punching power, even in the absence of skill, often secured victory for the fighter. The young pugilist Glaukos of Karystos won his first Olympic attempt on the strength of his punch, even after receiving numerous injuries in the process at the hands of more skillful opponents. It is interesting to note that Glaukos later gained fame for his sparring skill, no doubt the result of his narrow and painful first Olympic victory which must have convinced him to improve his technique.

Boxers trained in a specially-equipped room in the palaestra known as the *korykeion*, which featured various types of striking balls (*korykos*) suspended from the beams of the ceiling. This equipment was utilized by the Greek boxer in much the same manner as a modern boxer uses a striking bag for punching. It was a wine skin filled with fig seeds, meal, or sand, and was hung at head level. The boxer would hit it full force and allow it to slam him in the torso upon its rebound to toughen up the midsection. The medical writer Antyllus provides us with a guide a heavy bag workout:

> "Those undergoing training use both hands, at first gently, then more vigorously, so that they attack it as it swings away, and when it swings back at them they give ground as they are thrust out of the way by its force. Lastly they punch it away beyond arm's reach ... with a final effort after doing it all the violence they can, they hit away so hard that if they were not very careful they would be thrown off their feet by the rebound ... So it [the bag] can make the body muscular and give it tone, and it is a powerful exercise for the shoulders and the whole frame."

Other methods of training by Greek boxers included light sparring practice (*akrocheirismos*). The fighters wore padded gloves (*sphairai*) and earguards (*amphotides*) to protect the hands and head against injury. Boxers were also fond of a primitive form of shadow-boxing (*skiamachia*), which sometimes was accompanied by the playing of the flute since the ancients recognized the importance of rhythm in their physical activities.

Among ancient Greece's most famous boxers was Diagoras of Rhodes. He was recognized for his many victories, but was even more renowned for his personal boxing style. Diagoras was one to never duck away from a blow, and always played by the rules of the sport. Fans adored the grace and dignity he displayed in his bouts.

Boxer striking his opponent's groin area.
Greek vase, sixth century B.C.

At the 83rd Olympiad, Diagoras watched his sons attain victories in both the boxing and pankration competitions. In celebration of their accomplishment, his sons placed their crowns on his head and carried him on their shoulders to the roaring cheers of the crowds. To Diagoras, this was his most glorious moment, and while contemplating this, a voice from the crowd advised him to die now since there was nothing left but to ascend to Olympus and become a god. Ironically, Diagoras, while still held by his sons, dropped his head and quietly expired.

Another famed boxer was Melankomas of Karia. He had an unusual fighting style which earned him countless victories. He was never injured, and never hurt any of his opponents. It was his belief that to injure another, or be injured yourself, was to lack bravery. In many of his bouts, Melankomas would present such an elusive target that his opponents would become either so frustrated or exhausted that they would give up and admit defeat. What was so remarkable about his performance was that he never struck a single blow at them.

Theogenes, an early fifth century boxer and pankratiast, who hailed from the island of Thasos, reportedly scored the greatest number of festival wins. With as many as fourteen hundred victories, he had won distinction as one of Greece's most revered athletic heroes with two Olympic crowns, three Delphic boxing championships, a number of boxing victories at the Isthmus, and as many as nine Nemean boxing triumphs. As might be expected, Theogenes' history is full of legend and folklore, and he was worshipped as a deity after his death.

Ancient boxing appears to have been more dangerous and ferocious than its modern version. The spectators came to see blood, and blood is what they got. To have completed a career in the sport unwounded *(atraumatistos)*, was a rare feat in itself. Few Greek boxers of the era could boast of such an accomplishment.

PANKRATION

The brutal, bloody sport of **Pankration**, or in the Latin spelling *pancratium*, was first introduced into the 33rd Olympiad in the year 648 B.C. The term is derived from the Greek adjectives *pan* and *kratos* and is translated to mean "all powers" or "all-encompassing." One who competed in such an event was referred to as a *pankratiast*. Some refer to the sport by an older term, *pammachon*, which means "total fight." The Greeks believed that pankration was founded by a great Attican sports hero, Theseus, who combined his skills in both wrestling and boxing, in order to defeat the fierce Minotaur in the labyrinth. It would soon become the most spectacular and most demanding of all athletic events.

The term, itself, is pronounced either as pan-cray-shun or pan-crat-ee-on, depending on the preferred dialect of the Greek language spoken. In any case, pankration refers to an ancient combat sport based on martial technique and was essentially an all-out, no-holds-barred fight between two contestants. It integrated bare-knuckle boxing, kicking, and submission wrestling. Only biting and gouging were barred. Anything else went, although the tough Spartan contingent allowed these, too, in their local sports festivals. Victory was sought with little to no regard of the danger to the body or the life of one's opponent.

Some of the more popular pankration techniques included straight power punches, low kicks, elbowing and kneeing, arm locks and armbars, takedowns and throws, as well as numerous chokeholds. Another favored maneuver, known as *chancery*, involved grabbing an opponent by the hair and pulling him face-forward into an uppercutting fist or resounding knee strike. To many martial arts historians, pankration was, in essence, the "jujutsu" of classical Greece.

Kicking was an essential part of pankration, especially rising kicks to the stomach (called *gastrizein*), and powerful sweeps meant to take an opponent off his feet. Kicks above the belt were used sparingly against a standing opponent, with blows aimed to the head or face only when one's adversary was on the ground and too weakened to block or catch the attacker's foot. Due to this unique tactic alone, many combative experts credit pankration as the first comprehensive unarmed fighting system on record.

Pankratiast delivering a low front kick.
Imperial Roman bronze figurine.

There is no evidence of pankratiasts employing the stylized kicking methods seen in karate and taekwondo today. In other words, there were no side kicks, back kicks, or spinning-type kicks. When kicks were used at all, they were usually in conjunction with a hand technique or as a distraction to get inside of the opponent's defensive perimeter. From one Roman bronze, a pankratiast is depicted delivering a low kick with his heel to the opponent's knee. The obvious intent of the fighter is to break it. The frieze also displays perfect balance on the supporting foot with a lowering of his body weight as to deliver the attack with the body behind the blow. There also appears to be a simultaneous block and punching preparation. This is indicative of the high-level of technique that the Greeks had developed in their native combat form, even at this time.

A Roman pankratiast traps his rival's hand and drives his knee into the groin. At right, a fighter wearing the lethal caestus stands over his downed opponent.
Marble Roman relief, 2nd century B.C

Striking in pankration was quite extensive and not limited to the closed fist. There are many images of fighters striking one another with a multitude of hand weapons such as with one's open palm or extended thumb, outstretched fingers, downward chops, backfist blows, etc. The prevalent striking tool, however, was a lunging straight punch to the head since much of the boxing was long range. Although there is evidence from numerous existing wall frescoes of some infighting with hooks, uppercuts, and elbowing, most pankratiasts preferred to close with a grappling maneuver. This reflects another of pankration's principles: strike when fighting from a distance, grapple when you move inside.

The "lunge"

Pankratiast punching and kicking his opponent simultaneously.

Pankration bouts were extremely brutal and sometimes life-threatening to the competitors. Rules were minimal in number. As in all of the heavy events, there were no weight divisions and no time limits. Referees were armed with stout rods or switches to enforce the rules against biting and gouging. The rules, however, were often violated by some participants who, realizing they were outclassed by a heavier and stronger foe, would resort to such measures to escape being seriously maimed. A poet of the period dubbed one group of pankratiasts "the lions" due to their propensity for biting their opponents. The contest, itself, continued uninterrupted until one of the combatants either surrendered, suffered unconsciousness, or, of course, was killed.

The fighting arena or "ring" was no more than twelve to fourteen-foot square to encourage close-quarter action. The terrain on which the contestants waged combat was an area of soft, dug-up sand called a *skamma*. This skamma was obviously limiting to certain body maneuvers, such as rapid lateral movement, which contributed to the fact that size and strength became critical factors in pankration, as well as in the boxing and wrestling events.

From early accounts, descriptions of pankration vary widely since it took differing forms according to individual preference and body stature. Any attempt, however, to classify it as either a ground-combat style or an "upright" method would be futile. By today's standards, ancient pankratiasts might be described as grapplers who freely used strikes to subdue their opposition. Others liken it to a kickboxing form with a heavy grappling influence.

There are stories of epic pankration matches that consisted solely of kicks and punches, with little to no wrestling moves employed. This form, referred to as *ano pankration*, required the combatants to remain standing and was considered to be a safer version of the sport. It was used more for training or in preliminary bouts. The open-style, called *kato pankration*, was primarily used in the Games and was a much rougher form. The contest continued after the fighters went to the ground. It would be accurate to say that in the open style, the tall fighter with long reach relied primarily on hitting, whereas the shorter, thick-set man emphasized grappling. Either way, pankration featured a diverse offensive arsenal which proved appealing to Greece's top combat athletes.

"Pankratiasts," wrote Philostratus, a famous fight reporter in ancient Greece, "practice a hazardous style of wrestling. They must employ falls backward which are unsafe for the wrestler and grips in which victory must be obtained by falling. They must possess skill in various methods of strangling; they also wrestle with an opponent's ankles, and twist his arm, besides hitting or jumping on him, for all these practices belong to the pankration, where only biting and gouging are prohibited. The Spartans allow even these practices, but the Eleans and the laws of the games exclude them, though they approve of strangulation."

Whereas biting requires no comment, Aristophanes describes the prohibited "gouging" as digging the hands or fingers into an opponent's eyes, nose, mouth, or other tender body parts. Vividly illustrated in a vase painting, a pankratiast has inserted his thumb and finger into the opposing combatant's eye, and the official is hastening with an uplifted switch to punish this infraction of the rules. A similar scene appears in another illustration, where a pankratiast forces his hand into the mouth of his downed foe.

Fighters were paired with the drawing of lots from a silver urn. The winners of each match fought each other until only two remained for the final bout. The winner of the event was always undefeated. Pankratiasts became proverbial for those athletes who were both physically and mentally prepared for all events. They assumed a stance that allowed good defense as well as attack. Their fingers were curled, midway between closing their fist and leaving the hand open, and in this manner they were quick to punch or grab as the situation demanded.

Pankratiasts gouging each other's eyes. The referee at right flogs them for this violation.
Greek vase, 480 B.C.

Pankratiasts usually began a match by sparring with their fists and open hands. Preliminary maneuvers, called *krocheirismos*, were employed at the onset and each fighter had his favorite opening technique. Sostratos, of Sikyon, was known as "Mr. Fingertips" because he often tried to break his opponent's fingers at the beginning of a bout to secure an advantage. He was so successful with this trick that he won twelve crowns at Nemea and Corinth, three at Olympia, and two at Delphi.

Facing one another, the contestants attempted to bring one another heavily to the ground by grappling, hitting, kicking, or sweeping the legs. Another dramatic presentation of a pankration battle shows a fallen competitor bleeding profusely from the nose, while the markings of his opponent's blood-stained hands are visible on his back. His opponent has sprung upon him, grasping one arm with his left hand, and is preparing to finish him off with his cocked right fist.

The pankratiast on top throttles his foe's throat and pummels him into submission with his right fist.
Greek vase, 500 B.C.

Strangulation was not of the two-handed "throttling" variety, but primarily employed the forearm across the windpipe or carotid artery. One favored technique was the *klimakismos* (Greek: ladder trick), a move in which a fighter positioned himself onto his opponent's back, encircled him with his legs, and choked him from behind with his arms while simultaneously squeezing the abdomen with his legs. This tactic could be employed while both combatants were still on their feet, or while they were grappling on the ground. The Eleans were particularly well-known for their use of this technique, as well as other submission strangleholds.

A wrestler who was thrown to the ground was defeated, but a pankratiast might deliberately fall on his back (*hyptiasmos*) in order to throw his opponent more heavily, or to gain a better strategic position. These types of techniques are common in judo and are often referred to as "sacrifice" maneuvers. One such tactic was the stomach throw, whereby the pankratiast seized his adversary by the shoulders or arms and fell backwards, simultaneously planting his foot in his opponent's stomach to flip him forcefully over his head. The fighter who fell to the ground first was sometimes in a precarious position, for his opponent would take advantage of the situation and attempt to mount him, immobilizing him with his legs, leaving his hands free to strike him or apply a stranglehold. The fighter on the bottom would attempt to turn on his back and employ his arms and legs to protect himself.

Locks applied to an opposing pan-kratiast's limbs were employed for the sole purpose of forcing one's foe into submission. Dislocated ankles, knees, and elbows were common injuries suffered during a match. Opportunities for applying joint-locking techniques were more frequent when one or both of the fighters were engaged in ground combat, where the contest was normally decided. As such, the struggle on the ground was often long and complic-ated, with the competitors sometimes sprawling full length, sometimes on top of one another, and sometimes on their knees. It was this aspect of pankration to which Plato, himself an Olympic wrestler, objected, and which compelled him to omit it from his ideal state as useless for warfare since "it did not teach men to keep their feet."

The top fighter has secured an armlock on his opponent, and prevents him from escaping by trapping his leg with his own.
Greek bronze, Hellinistic era.

The aspiring pankratiast, along with the boxers, trained in the korykeion. In addition to the punch balls, there were larger sandbags, hung about two feet from the floor, for developing powerful low kicks, although some of the tougher disciples were rumored to practice their leg techniques against tree trunks to toughen their feet and shins. Conditioning advocated stamina exercises such as running, stretching, and neck and abdominal work, as well as *skiamachia* to sharpen a fighter's movements and timing. In this drill, pankratiasts flailed the air with their strikes and kicks, similar to a modern boxer who throws his hand combinations in front of a mirror. Again, Antyllus describes this training as follows: "The shadow boxer must use not only his hands but also his legs, sometimes as if he were jumping, at other times as if he were kicking."

Right: Top fighter has obtained the mounted position by straddling his legs about his opponent's stomach. He is depicted snaking his arm under the throat to end the contest with a choke.
Roman clay lamp, first century B.C.

Below: The standing pankratiast attempts to turn the opponent on his back by twisting the face and pulling his leg.
Greek vase, 500 B.C.

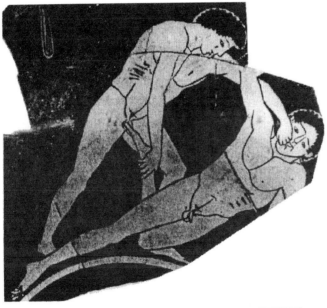

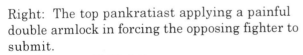

Right: The top pankratiast applying a painful double armlock in forcing the opposing fighter to submit.
Greek bronze, Hellinistic era.

Pankration was taught progressively to students, who were usually divided into pairs for training. Once an apprentice fighter had learned the basic moves and combinations of the art, he would be permitted to engage in open-sparring with other trainees. Sparring was emphasized to bring practice as close as possible to actual match conditions, but with light contact to avoid being injured prior to a contest. A pankration trainer, according to the orator Quintillian, will not teach his pupil "only to strike with fist or foot, or merely instruct him in a few wrestling holds, but he will coach him in every department of that event."

Surprisingly, pankration was considered less dangerous than Greek boxing. While serious injuries and fatal accidents did sometimes occur, they were rare in comparison to those in boxing. Greek combat athletes who entered both events in a single Olympiad would fight in the pankration first, so as not to "spoil themselves" for boxing. This was not because pankration was less threatening. On the contrary, the problem was that those who competed in boxing would end up with bloody gashes on his body, and this would no doubt hamper his performance in the pankration. On the other hand, a skilled pankratiast could survive the barehanded contact without bloody wounds that would slow him down in the boxing bouts. Nonetheless, the punishment incurred in the all-out combat matchup was such that the fighter who won both that contest and the boxing competition, usually captured the latter event by *akoniti* (Greek: default) when his impressive showing in the pankration cowed the prospective boxers into withdrawing.

Pankratiast on the right grabs his opponent by the arms while attempting to sweep his feet from under him.
Greek vase, 480 B.C.

Some formidable fighters were able to excel in all three combative events. One such athlete, Cleitomachus of Thebes, was celebrated in an epigram after winning the triple victory at the Olympic games of 216 B.C.: "Immediately after taking off his blood-soaked gloves, he fought in the fierce pankration." This was after Cleitomachus had already defeated all comers in the wrestling event which was held earlier.

The exploits of the ancient pankratiasts became legendary in the annals of Greek athletics. Stories abound of past champions who were considered invincible beings, even to the extent that their feats rivaled the mythology of the gods. Arrichion, Dioxxipus, Herakles, and Polydamos are among the most recognized names, their accomplishments defying the odds by besting armed opponents in life-and-death combat, and battling and killing wild animals when human competition was no longer a feasible challenge.

Perhaps the most famous, although fatal, account was recorded by Philostratus during the early days of the sport. It describes the renown champion, Arrichion of Phigaleia, who died and "won" at the same time. While being choked with the ladder trick, he twisted the challenger's ankle out of the socket with his last ounce of strength. The opponent raised his hand in submission as the winner expired.

The story of the Athenian Dioxxipus is another striking example of a trained pankratiast's skill. During a drinking party in the camp of Alexander the Great, a Macedonian warrior by name of Coragus challenged the Athenian, himself a pankration victor at Olympia in 336 B.C., to a duel. A day was appointed for the fight and thousands of soldiers came to watch, each expecting a one-sided contest favoring their fellow soldier. The Macedonian was fully armed and armored while Dioxxipus, as befitting a Greek athlete, stood naked and oiled, and wielding only a club. Coragus first hurled a javelin, which Dioxxipus dodged, then jabbed with a spear, only to have his opponent smash it with his club. Finally, as Coragus reached for his dagger, Dioxxipus grabbed Coragus' hand forcing him off-balance, and then swept his feet from under him. Dioxxipus completed his conquest by placing his foot upon his foe's throat while raising his club in a gesture of victory to the astounded onlookers.

Pankratiast on top punches at his adversary's face in an attempt to gain release from a tight headlock.
Greek vase, 500 B.C.

There are many stories of Herakles. Legends concur that he killed the feared Nemean lion by strangling it, since its hide was impenetrable by strikes. Vase paintings show him executing a shoulder throw on the beast, as well as a standing headlock. Herakles also defeated Antaios, the son of Earth, who constantly drew sustenance from his mother during contests against his adversaries. According to Pindar, Antaios was a barbaric ogre who fought invited guests, killed them, and then buried their bodies in his palaestra. In their encounter, Herakles, although dwarfed by his much larger opponent, was

31

able to terminate the life of Antaios by simply lifting him completely off the ground. This triumph marked the success of Hellenic skill over a savage who relied on magic for his strength.

Right: Herakles throwing the Nemean lion over his shoulder.
Greek vase, 530-515 B.C.

Left: Herakles trips Antaios backward by lifting his ankle out from under him, and bringing the fight to the ground.
Greek vase, 515-500 B.C.

    Still another famed pankratiast, Polydamos of Scotussa in Thessaly, was known to have fought and killed the Immortals, three of the royal bodyguards of a Persian king who had invited the champion athlete to Susa to perform an exhibition of his skill. In what was supposed to be a friendly match, Polydamos' opponents attempted to defeat him at the same time, only to meet their deaths.

    Exhibitions of superhuman strength were common, with boxers and pankratiasts often smashing stones and planks with their bare fists and driving their hardened feet through forged war shields. There are references in many Greek myths to a fire that burns in the depths of a man's soul, and when it burns brightly enough, makes him almost god-like in his abilities. This internal energy was called *pneuma*, and was theorized to be the essence of a champion pankratiast's extraordinary skill.

Pankration continued to be practiced until the early centuries of the Christian era, but as it entered the Hellenistic period, when Greece lost its independence, certain negative elements would cause the decline of the sport. This was due in part to its more violent characteristics, but principally because of the advent of professionalism. An excess of purses and honors to the athletic champions of all Greek sports had brought about social complications. The corruption inherent in professional athletics were considered worse in boxing, wrestling, and pankration, in particular. This so-called "evil" was increased by the absence of weight divisions which made these contests the monopoly of the heavyweight athlete. Consequently, the matches became less scientific and more brutal.

The greatest military leaders of ancient Greece disapproved of combat sports and pankration in particular. It was frequently criticized because of its emphasis on groundwork and sacrifice-type moves. Nonetheless, martial arts skills, including those utilized in the pankration, were a significant force in military training. Historical accounts of Sparta with its great battles of Marathon and Thermopylae against neighboring aggressors attest to the weaponless fighting skills of the trained soldier. Even grossly outnumbered, the Greek combat units fought tenaciously with sword, spear, and shield. And those who were disarmed continued empty-handed. Since penetrating the armor with one's blows was sometimes not an option, the warrior focused his assault on the neck and limbs of the opponent, applying proper body mechanics and leverage to either disable or kill him.

Pankration was basic to the majority of the Greek *hoplites* (foot soldiers) who served under the Macedonian Alexander the Great during his invasion of India in 326 B.C. Many authorities now contend that this dispersal of pankration techniques throughout the subcontinent laid the foundation for the countless Asian martial arts which evolved soonthereafter, including Chinese kung fu, Okinawan karate, and Japanese jujutsu. The subject has been one of controversy and conjecture for many years. In the West, it has always been a well-established fact that the Greek fighting arts spawned the American sports of boxing and wrestling as we know them today.

Perhaps the demise of the ancient Hellenic combatives was also due to the lack of an underlying philosophy strong enough to have prevented them from becoming mere spectacles as opposed to true art forms. What resulted was a gradual loss of the old ideals of *arete* (meaning martial value) or *aidos* (meaning honor) inspired by the Greeks. Thus, what began as an essential part of a warrior's training and flourished as a challenging sport, wound up as a corrupt and discredited form of prizefighting. Even so, pankration never completely vanished. Variations would appear from time to time in Greece but they resembled pale shadows of the original form, with the fighters now clothed in trunks and the addition of groin strikes to the list of enjoined techniques. Its popularity, especially in the nineteenth and twentieth centuries, would take a back seat to wrestling which the Greeks considered a much safer sport. It is accurate to say that Greco-Roman wrestling survives as a legacy of the ancient art.

One cannot, however, deny the significance of pankration as a comprehensive martial art of antiquity. It was, in fact, an almost limitless system, its broad spectrum of techniques bridging the gap between striking and grappling. As such, pankration reigns as the preeminent combat form of the ancient world.

II/THE EVOLUTION OF MODERN PANKRATION

In the process of development and improvement, many martial arts styles and derivations have evolved from the old. After years of intense training and investigation, the best of carefully selected fighting techniques were assembled and modified into a single system. Added to this was modern training methodology and principles of kinesiology (body mechanics). But the concepts of the classic art remained the main ingredient, actually the thread that held this mix together. This, in essence, was the birth of the μ (mu) τ (tau) style of pankration which evolved in the early 1970s. The Greek symbols, or mu tau, represent *Martial Truth* -- a preparation, both physically and psychologically, for the unrestrained and unpredictable conditions of a street-fight. Mu tau pankration is abbreviated as MTP. In essence, the MTP "curriculum" consists of:

MU TAU PANKRATION COMPONENT ARTS
- **Western Boxing**
- **Greco-Roman & Free-Style Wrestling**
- **Boxe Francaise Savate**
- **Muay-Thai Kickboxing**
- **Combat Judo**

MU TAU PANKRATION TECHNICAL ELEMENTS
- **Punching, striking, and elbowing techniques**
- **Kicking and kneeing techniques**
- **Takedowns, throws, and sweeping techniques**
- **Submission holds and joint locking techniques**
- **Submission chokes and strangulation techniques**

MU TAU PANKRATION TRAINING METHODOLOGY
- **Endurance training**
- **Strength training**
- **Striking tool development training**
- **Skills applications training**
- **Sparring**

Based on these characteristics, the following are some of the most significant features of this modernized pankration-based system:

- *Fluid readiness position.* MTP emphasizes a well-braced stance which allows for elusive motion, and is adaptable to either boxing, kicking, or grappling techniques.
- *Motion economy in defense and attack.* There is no wasted time or movement in MTP. Practitioners apply their offensive tools, parries, evasions, and blocks with minimal effort and turn defense into instantaneous attack.
- *Ranges of combat.* Modern pankratiasts recognize three basic combat ranges: long (kicking) range, medium (punching) range, and infighting range where elbows, knees, and grappling techniques are employed. The MTP offense is not limited by stylized preferences, but is TOTAL. The practitioner is equally skillful as a boxer, kicker, or grappler. He poses a dangerous threat from any distance, unlike some stylists who favors hands over feet, or prefer to fight at long range from his adversary.
- *No high kicks.* Pankration has long emphasized low-line kicks to the opponent's shins, knees, thighs, and midsection. These techniques are "safer" to execute than high kicks, which tend to leave you off-balance and vulnerable to attack. Kicks to the face or head from an upright position are reserved more for training than for actual combat.
- *Heavy use of training equipment.* Modern pankratiasts make ample use of striking shields, heavy bags, focus gloves, double-end speed bags, safety padding and headgear since such equipment allows for more realistic practice, as well as better power and speed development. This equipment enables practitioners of this fighting art to strike with full force against a moving target.
- *Focus on suddenly closing the gap.* One of the key elements in MTP is to spot an opening and immediately close the distance to make the transition to infighting range. From here, the modern pankratiast will often clinch with his opponent, delivering a barrage of elbow and knee blows, and initiate takedowns to force the action to the ground. In this position, "stand-up" fighters will be unfamiliar with the combat conditions since their punches and kicks are rendered useless.
- *Emphasis on grappling skills in close.* Although punches, kicks, and strikes are part of the mu tau arsenal, it has long been believed in pankration that the majority of fights will end up on the ground, where grappling techniques will be more effective than hitting. It is our contention that punching and kicking skills are **not** enough for the realities of the street.
- *Functional attack tools.* MTP techniques are based on simplicity and efficiency. There are no flashy, complicated moves such as spinning kicks or flowery hand movements. Full-power kicks to the legs, hard punch combinations, elbows and knees, submission chokeholds and arm locks are the modern pankratiast's primary tools. When necessary, gouging the eyes and hair-pulling, are utilized to assist in subduing one's opponent. Perfect form is secondary to causing maximum damage and resolving the conflict swiftly.
- *Reality training.* Street-practicality, not tournament fighting, is stressed in MTP. Pankration has always been a rough and tumble art, with training geared to simulate actual fight conditions as closely as possible. It does not waste time on unrealistic prearranged patterns or forms (i.e. kata). Sparring with full-contact and protective gear is the ultimate learning experience. Mu tau pankration encourages adaptability rather than memorized response to deal with the unpredictability of real combat.

- *Spartan conditioning.* Conditioning exercises to develop strength and endurance have always been stressed in the pankratiast's development. Weight resistance training, rope-jumping, and running long distances are included in MTP workout sessions to equip the practitioner with the physical attributes necessary to outlast and overcome the opposition.

Mu tau pankration can be considered "new wave" martial arts, if you will. Unlike a conventional Asian martial art with its emphasis on ritual and prearranged drilling (kata, one-step sparring, etc.), MTP stresses *adaptability* rather than memorized response. In this art, a technique's utility is determined ultimately through full-contact sparring, simulating realistic combat conditions. All of its teachings are geared to this end, free of the superfluous and the unessentials, and streamlined into the purely functional. The pankratiast is one who never meets every situation according to a predicted pattern, but reacts spontaneously, improvising his approach and tactics according to the uncertain actions presented by his opponent.

Although a contemporary art, mu tau preserves the Greek tradition of athleticism. In our way of thinking, a martial art is first and foremost an athletic endeavor, and not some mystical experience that gives one devastating powers. We also emphasize the importance of realism in training. To learn fighting requires that you fight, and become cognizant of all those aspects that a real fight is comprised of. While I will admit that even a street-fight cannot be completely duplicated within any martial art due to its unpredictability, pankration has always attempted to simulate it as closely as possible.

One must also learn to wage combat on the ground. This is certainly where most outcomes of a real fight are decided, and the practitioner must be well-versed in grappling skills to overcome his opponent from this position. Upright styles which emphasize kicking and punching will be useless on the ground if they are not schooled in ground tactics. A proficient grappler can easily get inside one's arms and legs and wrestle him down. This point has been proven over and over again, stretching from the ancient Greek Olympic games to the no-holds-barred combat events of today.

MTP is a distinct art -- the expression of oneself in combat. Essentially, the *style* does not make the man. Man, with his unique traits, determines the effectiveness of any style. The goal of the mu tau pankratiast is to be a well-rounded fighter. He is trained to be effective in either an upright posture or on the ground, against single or multiple opponents, and in both unarmed or armed situations. In a one-on-one situation, grappling and going to the ground might be the main strategy. However, against more than one opponent or in facing a weapon, the striking aspect may be favored. Everything depends on the circumstances; the mu tau pankratiast will adapt accordingly.

In summary, then, mu tau pankration can be described as an exclusive combat system, a Westernized martial arts hybrid whose theme is total fighting freedom. Its technical framework is highly eclectic, with various elements drawn from a number of other established combative systems. Each was liberally "borrowed" from to enhance the nucleus art of classic pankration. Not merely a blending of techniques, this system preserves a history and philosophy of ancient Greek athletics. And while it may be highly similar to other styles on the surface, it has a unique conceptual base etched in ancient Hellenic civilization, fusing skill, discipline, and Spartan tradition to a way of life. For this reason alone, mu tau stands as the first modern form of Greek pankration of its kind.

III/UPRIGHT COMBAT SKILLS
(Ano Pankration)

Fighting from a stand-up style, which favors striking techniques, is referred to in Greek as *ano pankration*. This important aspect of the art consists of the following elements: the ready position, footwork, distancing, angling, offensive strikes and kicks, and defenses.

READINESS POSITION

The basic premise in pankration is that all fights commence from an upright position, but frequently end on the ground. The readiness position, then, can be defined as the starting point for all defense and attack. It is a standup pose made up of the **on-guard** and the **stance**. Whereas the on-guard refers to the placement of the arms and hands, the stance is the positioning of the feet and trunk.

The stance features an upright posture with the feet placed slightly farther than shoulder width apart. If the fighter is right-handed, he places his right hand and foot in front. This is referred to as the *southpaw* position. With the left hand and foot forward, the fighter assumes the *orthodox* position. The front foot is flat on the ground with the rear foot focused on the ball, keeping the heel elevated about three inches to promote quick, springy-like movement. The knees are always slightly bent with one's weight equally distributed on both legs. A well-balanced but mobile stance is the main characteristic of a modern pankratiast's ready pose.

The torso should be turned sideways in most cases with the lead shoulder facing the opponent. By angling in this manner the midsection is protected, and greater reach is added to the lead striking weapons. The chin is tucked into the chest for protection, and the eyes should be on one's opponent at all times, looking into his upper chest. This enables you to see any movement executed with either hands or feet.

The placement of the feet is transitory, depending on the actual technique that is executed. For example, when punching, the modern pankratiast assumes more of a boxing stance, with the torso angled more toward the opponent. In round kicking, which is the dominant mu tau kicking tool, the body more squarely faces one's adversary. This allows for a quicker and more powerful delivery of the kicking leg. Once the grappling range is entered, the position of the feet may be altered again with a lowering of the center of gravity to gain more leverage to apply forceful takedowns and other maneuvers.

The fists should be held high at about chin height. A common error is to drop the lead arm, leaving the entire midsection and the head exposed. Just as dangerous is holding both hands below chin level. The upper body leans slightly forward at the waist (not the shoulders) to help cover and tighten the abdominal muscles. In addition to body protection, tilting forward brings you closer to your opponent, which enhances your power, reach, leverage, and accuracy in punching.

Southpaw Position (front view)

Southpaw Position (side view)

Orthodox Position (front view)

Orthodox Position (side view)

These upper body positioning concepts are much more effective than standing militarily erect with the head up and back straight all of the time. Such a position often tends to find the fighter backing away from blows rather than holding his ground and retaliating. Staying within striking range is essential to the pankratiast's offensive efficiency.

FOOTWORK

A modern pankratiast's footwork is best described as being light, loose, and "springy." A fighter should never move flatfooted, but should be up slightly on the balls of his feet, alert and ready to shift direction in a split second. Movement must be smooth and economical. Quick, nimble footwork is essential to successful scoring of one's kicks and punches, as well as moving in quickly to execute takedowns. If one's footwork is slow, the tools will be hard-pressed to accomplish their objective.

Good footwork is stressed in MTP and is used for three purposes:

1) *Defensive Footwork*
To present an elusive target for the opponent, one which is extremely difficult to hit or grab hold of. For example, lateral movement takes the body out of the direct line of fire.

2) *Offensive Footwork*
To move in on the opponent, to suddenly and explosively bridge the gap (close the distance) to execute one's attacks.

3) *Strategic Footwork*
To move around the opponent, searching for openings while maintaining a distance where you are safe and he is not.

DISTANCING

Distancing, or the spacial relationship between combatants, is critical to any fighter. In mu tau pankration, we recognize two distinct ranges: *striking range and grappling range*. The striking range is for upright fighting, and is broken down further into long, medium, and infighting. Each range is considered equally important, and the fighter must be able to cope with the conditions presented at both of these distances, and turn them to his advantage.

STRIKING RANGES

Long Range

Perhaps the safest upright striking range is the long range. This distance enables the pankratiast to deliver kicking techniques with his longest weapons, his legs. At this distance, the major function of the hands is for either deceptive purposes or defense. This range is not considered the primary fighting distance in pankration.

Medium Range

Next is the medium range, in which boxing techniques play a dominant offensive role. Straight line blows such as the lunging jab, extended-finger strike, and reverse thrust are employed from this range.

Infighting Range

The third and final upright striking range is the infighting range. This position features the more compact punching techniques, such as hooks and uppercuts, in addition to neck grabs, and lethal elbow and knee strikes.

GRAPPLING RANGE

The grappling range is perhaps the favored fighting distance in pankration. Once the fighters have closed the gap and go into a clinch, the action will almost always go to the ground where the strategy of the trained pankratiast is to end the conflict.

ANGLING

Angling refers to the exact strategic location from which to execute an attack or defend against oncoming blows or head-down charges. MTP recognizes three specific angles, each determined by the body positioning of both fighters. A skillful pankratiast will always attempt to find his opponent's weaknesses while avoiding his strengths. The proper angle depends to a great degree on the stances employed by the combatants. Each man will try to offset his foe's timing and sense of rhythm by constantly varying his positional angles.

UPRIGHT STRATEGIC ANGLES:

Direct Angulation

The fighter, regardless of stance, is positioned in front of the opponent.

Outside Angulation

The southpaw fighter positions himself to his LEFT of the opposing right-stancer; to his RIGHT of the orthodox stancer.

The orthodox fighter positions himself to his RIGHT of the opposing left-stancer; to his LEFT of the southpaw stancer.

Inside Angulation

The southpaw fighter positions himself to his RIGHT of the opposing right-stancer; to his LEFT of the orthodox stancer.

The orthodox fighter positions himself to his LEFT of the opposing left-stancer; to his RIGHT of the southpaw stancer.

Rear Flank

This positioning is the perfect placement from which to attack one's adversary, and is referred to as "attacking the blind side." A wide assortment of strikes, takedowns, and finishing holds can be administered from this position, be it while standing or on the ground.

STRIKING TOOLS

Mu tau pankration striking techniques are comprised of any blow with the open hand, closed fist, elbow, foot, shin, or knee. These blows are applicable from either an upright posture or when both fighters are waging combat on the ground. They consist of punching, gouging, elbowing, kicking, and kneeing.

The hands are the major close-range striking tools. Of these techniques, there are four basic punches, each of which having specific advantages in terms of angles and distances. Some punches are classified as minor blows in that, while they are not ordinarily designed to inflict severe damage to an opponent, they function to set up a major or knockout blow, or follow-up grappling maneuver.

HAND TECHNIQUES

The Lead Jab

The lead jab is perhaps the most important hand tool in mu tau pankration. It is a straight line blow aimed primarily to the opponent's face. It is used as the initial strike or feint in almost every punching flurry, and it closes the distance for the harder blows as well as grappling takedowns. It is also used for stopping an oncoming attack. The jab is delivered with the forward hand and makes a quarter-turn to land on its target horizontally. Attempting to land jabs to the body is rare, as bending forward to hit to this area increases the risk of running into a counterpunch or elbow strike.

The jab can be delivered while the fighter remains well-covered by the rear hand. This is important in the eventuality of a blow missing its mark. It is often a wise strategy to deliver multiple jabs since the second or third one has a chance of landing even after the first has missed. Sustained jabbing keeps the opposing fighter on the defensive and constantly off-balance.

Two types of jabs are used: a quick, snappy strike with quick retraction, or a stiff jab which carries greater body force and follow-through. Both blows are delivered with a "lunge", a long, quick step or shuffle forward from medium range.

Lead jab with lunge step.

Lead jab to face.

The Extended-Finger Strike

This hand technique is much like the lead jab punch but with the fingers extended. The sole target is the eyes, and is designed to incapacitate the opponent by blinding him. The use of the finger strike, as a serious self-defense weapon, abides by the old Greek adage that "if one cannot see you, he cannot hit you." The blow employs the front hand, with the first three fingers curled into a point and the thumb held in. Speed and accuracy, not power, are the essential elements in this attack. With the shorter distance it has to travel to

46

reach its mark and the added three or four inches in reach, the extended-finger strike is considered a highly-efficient tool in the modern pankratiast's offensive arsenal.

Extended finger strike.

Due to its simple body mechanics and quickness, the finger strike enables the fighter to maintain good balance at all times. As a result, it is often utilized as a sustained assault and for setting up other techniques.

Leading finger strike to opponent's eye.

Reverse Thrust

Also called the rear cross, this hand tool is classified as a power punch in MTP. It is a straight-line punch utilizing the rear hand, and is delivered chiefly to the head in the form of a counter, as a follow-up to a feint, or as the finishing stroke in a punching combination.

The technique derives considerable power from the greater distance it has to travel to its target and the fact that you have the full weight of the body behind the blow. Power comes from a swivel of the hips and a pivot on the ball of the back foot. The punching fist makes a quarter turn in its delivery and lands horizontally on its mark. The leading hand protects by folding back by the chin to cover and deflect return punches if necessary.

Rear thrust to opponent's face.

48

Hook Punch

The hook is a short, crushing blow which travels outside of the opponent's line of vision in a circular motion to attack the chin, side of the head, the solar plexus, or ribs. Primarily an inside range tool, the hook is employed as a strong counter or follow-up blow which often catches an opponent moving in. In extremely close quarters, the hook can also function as an effective lead when your adversary sports an airtight guard which cannot be penetrated by straight-line blows. Usually, the hook follows other maneuvers such as a feint or lead jab in order to obtain the best leverage.

The hook is never a wide, looping movement, but is a compact blow, one that travels no more than eight to ten inches. Power is supplied by getting the shoulder and hips into the punch. The hand should not telegraph that it is on the way by withdrawing, winding up, or lowering prior to delivery. The body simply turns away from the arm until the play of the shoulder joint is used to the limit.

High lead hook.

Lead hook to opponent's jaw.

The secret to powerful hooking is leverage - shifting the weight of the body behind the blow at the exact moment of impact. Maximum body weight will be transmitted into the punch with the arm serving as the conductor of the force. Potent hooks are NOT arm punches; they are the result of maximizing one's own body weight into the attack.

Low lead hook.

Lead hook to head.

Either hand is utilized in hooking, although the lead is favored. Most hook punches are also directed to the head. The lead hook to the body is executed by bending the front knee so the shoulder is on line with the target. The rear hand is positioned high to shield the face and the elbow is held tight to the body to protect the ribs. The chin should be positioned behind the lead shoulder to avoid being tagged by a rear cross counter or elbow attack. All of the weight is over the front foot as the fighter pivots into the blow. The hand "digs" at an angle into the ribs or solar plexus.

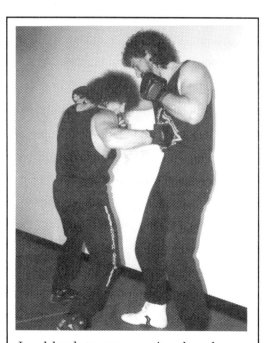

Lead hook to opponent's solar plexus.

The rear hook is very similar in delivery to the lead hook, except that the puncher twists his back foot to gain power. The rear heel lifts as the weight of the body is transferred to the front leg. The rear hook is primarily a head shot, although it is sometimes used to the body.

High rear hook.

Low rear hook.

Rear hook to opponent's body.

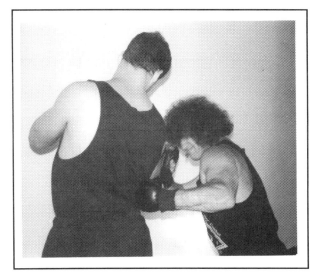

Rear hook to opponent's jaw.

Uppercut

Like the hook, the uppercut is a potent close range punching tool. It is best used against an opponent who moves in close with head down charges, or one who favors crouching and staying low in his on-guard position. This technique is not very useful against the upright fighter who prefers jabbing and kicking from a relatively safe distance. Actually, the uppercut is a form of the hook except that it is delivered upward instead of sideways. It features a scooping motion with the palm facing you and can be administered with either hand. The targets are the point of the jaw, the face, ribs, and solar plexus.

Lead uppercut to chin.

Lead uppercut to opponent's chin.

Lead uppercut to body.

Lead uppercut to opponent's solar plexus.

Rear uppercut.

CHANCERY

An ancient technique very popular when using the uppercut is **chancery**. This involves pulling the opponent's hair and jerking him face-forward into an uppercutting fist. The blow is delivered to either the chin or body.

Hairpull and uppercut to chin.   Hairpull and uppercut to solar plexus.

ELBOW STRIKES

The elbow strike (*Greek: agg-kohn*) is one of the most powerful and dangerous weapons in close-quarter standup combat. In modern pankration there are three basic techniques using the elbow for standup fighting: forward strike and downward strike. The downward elbow is also employed as a ground-striking tactic when the pankratiast has attained a position of controlling the opponent from being on top.

Elbow strikes are performed following the same theoretical principles as hand techniques. Power is generated by rotating the entire body behind the attack. They are never the starting blow in an attack, but usually are the second or third strike in a series. They frequently follow a lead jab. They are also effectively used as counters. The primary targets are the head and base of the neck. When toe-to-toe or from a clinch where the arms are trapped, the elbows can be freely utilized.

Elbow strikes should be practiced whereby the right elbow strike immediately follows the left elbow strike, and vice versa. These techniques are frequently executed by stepping forward slightly.

Due to the close range and speed, an elbow attack is difficult to defend against. The most common defenses include full-cover and forearm blocks.

Downward elbow strike.

Down elbow to base of neck.

KICKING TECHNIQUES

Pankration, considered the oldest complete combative sport on record, was one of the first, if not the first, to have included kicking techniques (*Greek: lak-tee-zo*) in its extensive arsenal of offensive tools. Evidence points to the fact that many of early pankration's kicks were aimed low, to the lower stomach and to the legs. Writings of the early Greek fight reporters also indicate the use of both the direct, or front, and round-type kicking movements. The latter technique was a favored means of sweeping the legs from under an opponent, and bringing combat to the ground where grappling and hitting were employed together so effectively by the Greek champions.

Further documentation also shows that the later adoption of pankration by Greek military units brought about new foot attack tools, such as an angular kick delivered very similar to the side kick seen in many modern karate styles as well as in French savate. Legend has it that some highly-skilled hoplites used this kick in battle to penetrate the war shields wielded by their enemies. In many museums around the world, there are vase paintings which depict Greek fighters kneeing and stomping upon a downed combatant during a contest.

The martial arts contain a number of flashy, complicated kicking maneuvers such as spinning and flying techniques, and multiple-kicking with the same leg. In pankration, such moves are never used as they lack the accuracy and power to wear down and damage the opponent. These kicks may certainly look impressive, but more often than not, they leave you off-balance and more vulnerable to being countered. They are more suited to a tournament or controlled environment than the serious conditions of a street brawl.

Although kicks are the primary long range artillery, they are not considered an emphasized attack, as they are in many Korean and Chinese martial arts styles. For the most part, kicking in pankration serves as either a prelude to or is used in conjunction with a hand technique. As with other striking techniques, kicks are also employed as a distraction to set the opponent up for a takedown.

Mu tau pankration's kicking weapons consist of the shod foot, the shin, and the knee. In using the foot, proper positioning in the various kicks is critical. Kicks will be unable to impart their full destructive force unless the foot is properly positioned. Proper foot positions absorb the shock of impact, preventing injuries such as broken toes and ankle sprains. The six weapons employed in modern pankration kicking techniques are as follows:

- **TOE (Point of Shoe).** Formed by curling the toes down. Used for lead and back-leg round kicks at longer range.

- **HEEL.** Formed by pulling the foot straight back. Used exclusively in the low side kick.

- **INSTEP.** Formed by curling the tip of the shod foot down. Used in lead and back-leg round kicks from longer range.

- **BALL OF FOOT.** The foot is kept straight with the toes pulled back tightly. Utilized exclusively when executing front thrust kicks.

- **SHIN**. The shin is the lower part of the leg used in round kicking techniques executed from closer range. Mu tau pankratiasts toughen this area to a great degree by kicking heavy bags repeatedly in training.

- **KNEE**. Used for close range combat. Either the front or side of the knee can be used.

Attacking the legs is emphasized in modern pankration. Leg kicks are both powerful and difficult to defend against. With a single successful attack all of the opponent's faculties - offense, defense, mobility - will simultaneously be impaired.

Leg kicks are usually used as first-stage attacks. They can lead into more complex offensives, they can be employed to "feel-out" an adversary, or they can keep an opposing fighter at a distance momentarily, gaining time and space for the next stage of attack. Whether it be part of a more complex strategy or not, a well-placed, full-powered leg attack can take down or disable even the best combatant.

The opponent's front leg is the primary target for the low kicks. As it is nearest to you, it is the easiest to reach as well as the slowest to leave striking range. The best time to attack the opponent's front leg is when he is either stationary or advancing since he will find it difficult avoiding the blow and his own momentum, if moving forward, may contribute to the impact. Areas of the leg to be attacked are the shin, knee, back of the knee, calf, and thigh. The downward side kick, and both the lead and back-leg roundhouse kicks are chiefly used in mu tau pankration leg attacks.

The list of kicking tools is six in number. The most functional foot tools are those directed toward the lower body and with a short, fast trajectory. It is a common tactic of pankratiasts to always try the simplest, most reliable techniques first, and if these do not work, only then go on to the more complicated.

Front Snap Kick to Groin

Pankratiasts have long used this foot attack for combat. The application of this kicking tool is very much like that of the lead jab punch. It can be used as a finishing kick, as the kick for creating openings, or in a series of hand and foot techniques. And like the jab, it utilizes the lead limb. There is no "chambering" to this technique, whereby the knee is raised high into the chest area prior to delivery. After sliding in with the rear foot, the front leg snaps from the lower leg at the opponent's

groin area. The tip of the shoe is the striking point.

Front Thrust Kick

The front thrust kick is similar to the front groin kick, except with more power. A slight chambering motion is employed in this technique enabling the hips to drive forward for greater penetrating force. The ball of the foot is used primarily to attack the lower stomach or in some cases, the kneecap. When delivered to the body, it is used more as a push to keep the opposing fighter at a distance. This is a favored kick to stop the opponent's back-leg round kick.

Front thrust kick to lower stomach.

Front thrust kick to opponent's knee.

Lead Round Kick

The lead round kick is delivered on a medium or low line with the point of the shoe extended. Its delivery features a short, outward step for greater hip rotation in the blow.

The supporting leg should be kept straight for medium round kicks, and bent for low round kicks. The knee faces the target with the foot extended along the cocked leg. The targets vary: ribs, solar plexus, stomach, and kidneys for medium-line round kicks; and the thighs for low round kicks. The thigh kick is a very common attack in pankration. As in any kick, the head can be attacked with the foot if the opposing fighter is on the ground, and clearly vulnerable.

Lead Round Kick to thigh.

EXECUTION OF LOW LEAD ROUND KICK

Readiness Positions. Pankratiast on right assumes southpaw stance.

Footwork in the maneuver involves crossing the left foot in front of the lead foot by stepping outward and pivoting on the supporting foot. The lead leg is chambered slightly.

Kick lands on outside of thigh as kicker completes pivot on ball of supporting foot.

Back-Leg Round Kick

In the back-leg round kick, the body pivots on the ball of the rear foot. Sometimes, an outward step precedes the pivoting motion, which enhances kicking force. In executing this technique, the kicking foot starts from a stance with the body more squared to one's opponent. With the arms and hands protecting the head and torso, the body pivots on the ball of the front foot with a simultaneous rotation of the hips. The kicking leg goes immediately to its intended target in an arc, with no chambering motion. The object is to fully turn into the kick and follow through with maximum penetration. This technique is more similar to Thai boxing than in karate or taekwondo which emphasizes an initial chambering action. It is delivered with the swing of the entire body, and not only with a snap of the lower leg. The instep or shin is used as the striking surface, depending on the distance, and the targets include the thigh and body.

EXECUTION OF BACK LEG LOW ROUND KICK

Readiness Positions. Pankratiast on left assumes orthodox stance.

Pankratiast on left pivots on ball of supporting front foot and swings his whole body behind his right leg. There is no leg chambering.

Kick lands on outside of thigh with full follow-through of turning body.

Back-leg round kick to opponent's body.

Back-leg round kick to head of opponent on the ground.

Side Kick

This is a powerful foot weapon, and is utilized as a full-powered thrust rather than a snap. It is delivered solely to the low line. The side kick is a quick and ravaging low line stamp designed to dislocate or snap an opponent's leg with a single well-placed blow. Best used with the slide footwork from the on-guard, the lead leg is thrusted straight out and down at the shin or kneecap in one fluid motion. A useful prelude to the move is a distracting, upward feint with the forward hand. Contact is made with the bottom of the foot or heel. Due to the potential force of this kick, the outside foot edge or blade is not used since a broken foot could easily result.

63

Offensively, the downward side kick is almost impossible to block. In the street, the average brawler would not expect it and has no adequate defense against it. Logically, it is the best offense to apply at the onset of a fight. The shin and knee are the targets located closest to you and since they are exposed, they are difficult to protect. Also, the downward side kick is a good means of bridging the gap to employ combinations.

Defensively, this kick can be used to stop almost any kind of oncoming strike or kick. The concept of the defensive application is to beat your adversary's timing with your superior leg reach. You must attempt to intercept your opponent while he is in motion and fully committed, just before or during the moment he is launching his blow. The downward side kick is highly effective for this purpose as it utilizes the longest weapon to the nearest open target.

Downward sidekick to opponent's knee.

The downward side kick is not only a very powerful kick but is a relatively safe tool to employ. Since the side of your body faces the opponent throughout the maneuver, very few of your most vital targets are ever exposed to his attack. The kick also offers a secure distance outside of the opponent's fist range.

Sidekick to shin against jab to face.

Knee Kick

The use of the knee (Greek: gyo) provides the MTP combatant with a dangerous infighting weapon. There are two types of knee kicks employed instinctively by fighters once they clinch or are able to grab each other about the neck: front knee kicks and round knee kicks. The primary targets are the contained head and body, and the part of the leg above the knee.

Once a firm grasp about the neck is secured, the mu tau pankratiast has been trained to unleash a series of devastating knee attacks, with either the leading leg or back leg, into his opposition. Surviving such an onslaught requires not only the highest level of skill, but superb physical fitness. Knee strikes are delivered with the lower leg pulled back, toes pointed down, and the

upper body leaning away at a 45-degree angle. Following these principles provides protection against head shots while employing knee strikes in close.

Knee kick to opponent's face.

Knee kick to opponent's ribs.

Applying a **neck clinch** is an integral part of an effective knee attack. Clinching allows the fighter to control his adversary while keeping him close enough for the knee to land solidly and accurately. It is important that from this close range one's head is never dropped, as this will open the face up to the opponent's knee technique. The fighter must also make certain to keep the elbows close together. The hands are crossed high on the opponent's head and the forearms are used for leverage to pull him forward into the knee.

NECK GRAB AND KNEE EXECUTION

The knee can also be employed to attack the leg area at the thigh. Rather than grabbing the neck, however, the pankration is trained to clinch the opposing fighter about the waist when applying this technique.

Knee kick to opponent's thigh with waist clinch.

Key points in MTP striking/kicking execution:

- For speed and accuracy, all striking techniques must be executed from the ready position without winding up, to avoid telegraphing or giving away the intended action.

- After completing a punch or kick, the striking limb must be immediately retracted to the readiness or on-guard placement.

- The shoulders and arms must be kept loose and relaxed when hitting; the muscles of the body contract only at the moment of impact.

- It is important to get leverage into every blow for maximum power. Effective punching and kicking is the result of using the entire body in the blow, not mere arm or leg strength alone!!!

- The rear or guarding hand is always positioned to protect the upper body from a counter. The rear hand does most of the defensive work and is a supplement to the other hand. If one hand is hitting, the other should be protecting the body. It is always in position, correlating to the uncovered line or unprotected area. And it is always tactically placed for an offensive follow-up.

- The rear hand is also used offensively but more as a counter or as part of a combination (following a lead jab, for example). More power is generated than with the forward hand due to the added distance and the fact that the full use of the body is employed behind the punch.

- Punching is practiced with economy of motion, accuracy, and from a variety of angles, both as singular blows and in combination. The goal is to be able to deliver one's blows in fluid series and to ultimately synchronize the punching techniques with all other attack tools.

- One must be careful not to initiate power blows such as hook punching, and elbow and knee strikes from too far out as it will make him vulnerable to counter-offensives.

- For maximum force and penetration, kicks should always be delivered with the upper body leaning slightly forward into the attack. The body should not lean back to upset one's balance and nullify the potential for follow-ups.

- The arms should be guarding the head and body during all kicks, and instantly ready to go on the offensive.

- Avoid these common errors in delivering jabs and hooks: lifting the rear foot off the ground; dropping your front shoulder; lowering the rear guard; or dropping the front hand after punching to create an opening.

DEFENSES

Although pankration has long been attack-oriented, a protective defense cannot be overlooked. Taking the tough-guy attitude of "I'll take a shot to give one", is NOT a very wise tactic and only serves to take its toll on a fighter. Coming away from a fight the victor, but still bloodied and hurt, is the strategy of the poorly-schooled combatant. Effective defensive skills were lacking in the earliest form of pankration, but through the passing of time and with modification, they have been developed to a high degree in its descendent art.

The following are the basic stand-up defensive techniques which are critical to the modern pankratiast's survival in upright fighting. It is essential to bear in mind that a fighter cannot begin to possess a potent offense until he has first mastered an air-tight defense.

Arm and Leg Blocks

The mu tau pankratiast is trained to maintain a tight guard with the hands close together at chin height and the elbows held close to the rib cage. From this position, one should be able to block a high percentage of the opponent's punches and elbow blows by taking them on the arms. Against close range hooks, the defender should cover with his rear arm. For defending against a power round kick, a raised knee against the shin or a straight knee angled inward to the inner thigh as the kick is delivered are the best defenses. These function as effective counters as well.

Rear arm block against hook to head.   Full cover against elbow to head.

Since low kicks are a favored offense in MTP, the fighter must also be well prepared against attacks below the belt line. Low round kicks aimed to the outer thigh are often blocked with a toughened shin. Frontal kicks aimed to the lower body are intercepted in flight at the sensitive shin with a partially-extended side kick (leg obstruction).

1. Readiness positions.

Shin block.

2. Jam front kick with sidekick to knee.

70

Parries

Parries are subtle, economical movements performed with a sharp slap of the palm to the inside, outside, or onto an oncoming blow or kick, with the intention of diverting the assault from its original path. Unlike the passive, rigid blocking techniques of some classical karate styles, the parry utilizes far less energy and allows redirection of force rather than absorbing a bruising bone-on-bone clash.

The key elements in the parry are timing and economy of motion. It is paramount to parry at the last moment (late rather than early), when the blow is close to the body. Reaching out to parry an attack not only causes openings for counterhits, but enables the opponent to alter the direction of his blow.

Either hand can be used to parry but never both at once. While one hand is deflecting the blow, the other hand (usually the front) is preparing to counter. As the parry is executed, it is often wise to swing the head and body slightly in the opposite direction of the strike. This provides one with extra assurance that the attack will pass by harmlessly. A skillful striker with an excellent sense of timing has the ability to parry and punch simultaneously.

Parrying is an excellent means of defending against a wide variety of blows, but is most effective for straight-line hits. Head shots can be parried to either the left or right, while blows aimed to the body are deflected downward. Front and side kicks can also be parried effectively by stepping back slightly or using lateral movement (sidestepping) to dissipate much of the kick's force. If executed perfectly, the parry can act to off-balance the opponent, placing him out of position to follow up with another attack.

Evasions

Another effective MTP defense is the evasion which allows the freedom of both hands to counter while remaining in the attacking range. Evasion is much like parrying where timing is so crucial. The movement is performed late rather than early, when the blow is almost upon you. In mu tau pankration, there are two basic evasions: slipping and ducking.

Slipping is a movement of the head to the inside or to the outside of a straight-line blow, usually a hand attack. Slipping is very bewildering to an opponent and keeps him uncertain about landing his own shots. It also causes him to use up his strength, as nothing in a fight is more tiring than missing blows due to the extra effort expended in recovering one's balance. On the other hand, by the use of the slip, one can avoid a punch with the least amount of exertion, and thus conserve strength and energy.

Inside slip.

Outside slip.

The most commonly used slips in MTP are those head movements to one side, just enough to let the punch pass by harmlessly. One does not change the position of his feet, but bends his upper body to the right or left, far enough to carry the head out of line and allow the blow to go over his shoulder. The fighter now finds himself in excellent position to unleash a blistering counterattack.

Outside slip against jab lead.

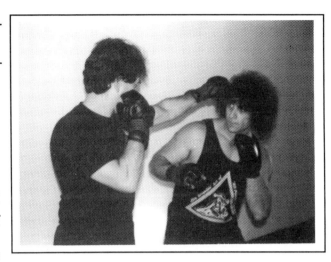

It is important to note that slipping is for leads to the head only. Body blows are taken on the arms, parried, or dodged. Also, a slip should never be initiated until the attack is on the way, as it may be a trick to fake you out of position.

Ducking is an evasive move for swings or hooks to the head by lowering the head so that the blow passes over it. It is an effective means of avoiding a blow at the inside hand range because an opponent is made to miss without losing your balance, thus leaving you in an advantageous position to counter.

The ability to duck well will improve one's fighting prowess. The man who can duck effectively is hard to hit squarely, and is generally able to fight closer to his opponent, always remaining within range for a countering strike or in most cases, a takedown.

The only blows that ducking should be attempted against are swings or hooking-type blows directed at the head. The technique of ducking does not involve bending at the knees. The fighter drops his body by bending forward at the waist. The guard is always brought in front of his face. Failure to do so will leave one vulnerable to uppercuts or knees to the face. A common ploy of the pankratiast is to avoid a head shot by ducking under it and to shoot for the legs to take the opponent down.

IV/STRIKING TOOL DEVELOPMENT USING EQUIPMENT

Equipment is an integral part of pankration training. Just as a piece of training apparatus improves the output of any athlete, the use of functional devices serves to sharpen the striking tools of the full-contact fighter. It is particularly useful when a partner is unavailable to work out with and it is an invaluable means for developing areas of weakness. Using a variety of devices, there is a systematic manner in which specialized fighting skills such as timing, power, speed, accuracy, distancing, balance, etc., can be enhanced.

In mu tau pankration, equipment is treated as a real opponent rather than just a target to pound on. Some of these devices offer movement, whereby one's precision in his blows are affected, as well as his timing to hit at the proper moment. Regardless of the type of apparatus utilized, it is imperative for the trainee not to forget about his guard when attacking, keeping himself well-covered at all times. It is also important that the person or training partner holding the equipment is adept in its manipulation. He should act as a coach and sometimes as an opposing fighter, forcing you to get the best possible workout and to be aware of areas that need improvement. He should make you move, cover up, and hit from all possible angles.

The primary equipment employed in modern pankration training include the heavy bag, the speed bag, the top-and-bottom bag, the focus gloves, the impact shield, the offense-defense (O-D) mitts, and the kick pads.

The Heavy Bag (korykos)

The heavy bag is one of the most important pieces of training equipment used in mu tau pankration tool development. Pankratiasts have long used the heavy bag, or *korykos*, to develop kicking and punching force. Although today's standard models weigh about 80 pounds, the heavy bags utilized in modern pankration training weigh approximately 150 pounds. There are even larger bags which are foam and water-filled and tip the scales at over 200 pounds. Some bags used in MTP training, referred to as "banana bags", are six feet in length.

The main purpose of the heavy bag is power. Any striking tool can be applied with full force to the bag, which is normally stabilized by a partner or tied down to the floor. When training with the bag, it is absolutely critical to

consider the bag as an opponent rather than just a "dead" object to beat on. Though it is incapable of hitting back, the pankratiast must keep his guard up and stay well-covered when attacking. By all means, one should use his imagination and treat the bag as if it is part of a real fight. Good movement, feinting, and variation in one's offense are emphasized in heavy bag workouts.

Mu tau pankration heavy bag training consists of three minutes of intense work followed by one-minute breaks. It is important for the student of this art to develop the capability of delivering fluid hand and foot combinations, although it is good practice to isolate certain techniques such as punching combinations, just kicks, or elbow and knee techniques, in some of the rounds.

The Speed Bag

The speed bag is an air-inflated leather bag that is attached by a swivel connection to an overhead rebound platform. The basic purpose of this apparatus is to develop speed of hand. In addition, it sharpens hand/eye coordination, timing, rhythm, and strengthens the shoulder muscles.

In a modern pankration palaestra, it is common to find speed bags of varying size. The physical stature, as well as the ability, of the trainee determincs to some degree the size of the bag that is appropriate. The larger bags require more powerful blows to make them move, whereas the smaller bags tend to move faster, thereby improving one's speed and coordination.

Due to the influence of western boxing on punching skills, mu tau pankratiasts are trained to use the speed bag in the same way that a conventional boxer does. Beginning students stick to practicing their punches individually, and the more advanced practitioners employ many different striking patterns with a high level of proficiency.

Drill time with the speed bag is normally two or three rounds with a minute break in between each round. The duration per round is three minutes.

The Double End Bag

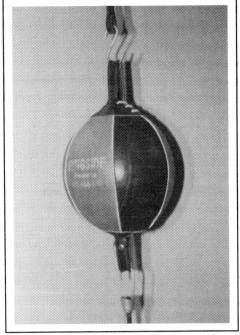

The double-end bag has been utilized in MTP training since its earliest beginnings. Inflated with air, the leather-covered bag is circular in shape and is suspended at shoulder or face level (or higher) by a pair of springy elastic cords attached to the ceiling and floor. It comes in various sizes: eight, six, or even four inches in diameter, the smaller, faster bag for the more advanced.

The double end bag is very difficult to hit consistently with any degree of accuracy at first. Unless it is struck perfectly straight and square, it will bounce back from an unpredictable angle. The harder it is hit, the quicker and more forceful it returns.

Next to a live sparmate, the top-and-bottom bag is perhaps the best means of developing your reflexes, timing, hand speed, and accuracy. Any type of strike is applicable: jabs, crosses, hooks, even uppercuts and elbows. Combination punches, primarily double jabs, the one-two, and the one-two-three, can also be employed once the mu tau-ist gains some experience in landing the single blows effectively.

As in the case of the heavy bag, this apparatus is treated by a pankratiast as if it is a real opponent. Good footwork is used to control the bag's elusive movement, and defensive moves are applied as well as attack. The bag is struck forcefully and is evaded with a head slip as it caroms back. One must be careful to maintain his cover and work the bag with a broken rhythm. In other words, it is not an objective to punch the bag with a set pattern of blows and timing. The attacks should vary with a continuous alteration in the tempo of one's actions.

Another version of this equipment used in mu tau pankration training is the double double-end bag, which offers two targets to strike as well as a different rhythm for the fighter to adapt to. This is ideal for developing high/low and low/high punching combinations.

Drill time is typically three rounds with a minute rest in between rounds. The duration of each round can be from three to five minutes, depending on ability.

Focus Gloves (punch mitts)

One of the most versatile and extensively used MTP training aids is the focus glove, which sharpens accuracy, timing, striking speed, and power in virtually any punch as well as some kicks.

The most effective use of the focus glove is in cultivating different punching (and kicking) combinations. In this drill, a holder wears gloves on both hands and continuously alters their positions, providing a constantly moving target. To get the most out of this type of training, you must work with a partner who is proficient in manipulating the gloves. He must keep you moving and persist in providing you with a variety of angles from which to strike. In modern pankration training, the holder functions as the "coach", and will call out combinations for the hitter to deliver, often using number sequences, such as one-two, one-two-three, etc.

Focus gloves come in various sizes. The smaller mitts are used primarily for punching drills, while there are larger sizes utilized for practicing elbow strikes. Drill time for focus glove training is variable. On the average, three rounds of three minutes each with the one-minute breaks are adequate.

Impact Shield

The impact shield is an apparatus filled with a dense foam core which is contoured in shape similar to the human body. Its design enables the trainee to strike it full force without it losing its original shape.

This device is used to sharpen the body attack. The mu tau pankration kicking tools employed are the front thrust kick, both the power lead and back-leg round kick, and kneeing. Punching techniques used include the reverse thrust, and hooks and uppercuts with either hand. The

partner holding the equipment positions the shield firmly to his chest and moves about rapidly, in and out, as well as laterally, providing a moving target for one's strikes. He will also rush in frequently without warning forcing a spontaneous reaction on the hitter's part.

Drill time with the impact shield is two to three rounds or three to five minutes each. The trainees rest one minute between rounds.

O-D (Offense-Defense) Mitts

The O-D mitts are used to sharpen the offensive hand tools while simultaneously teaching good defensive skills such as covering, slipping and ducking. The value in this equipment is in forcing the puncher to concentrating on keeping well-guarded at all times. The "coach" will lead and counter with jabs and other blows to assure that his partner fluidly integrates defense with attack.

Kick Pads

The kick pads are used by the modern pankratiast to harden the shins and knees. Full-power, follow-through round kicks with either leg are heavily favored techniques, although knee attacks are also practiced. For hard kick-punch combinations, the kick pad can be worn on one arm with a focus glove on the other hand.

The pads are leather arm shields about one foot in length and filled with a dense foam. A rigorous session with this rock-hard equipment will leave the kicker bruised and swollen. Fitted with top handles and forearm straps, they are worn by a partner who defends against solid round kicks to both the lower and upper body. He will turn the pads into each kick to offer greater resistance, thereby increasing the impact. The holder of the pad may also reach out occasionally with one of the mitts to tap the kicker in the head if his guard is too low. Even on the attack, the fighter must be aware of his defense. It is the trainer's responsibility to see to it that this lesson is properly learned.

In practicing the knee kicks, the hitter will grasp the holder at the sides of his head in a clinch. The holder crosses the pads at his stomach and absorbs the pounding of multiple knee strikes while at the same time resisting the kicker's downward pull. If this was actual combat, the grip works not only to pull the head down where it can be assaulted with the knees, but also as a chokehold, reducing the flow of blood to the brain and further weakening the opponent. This training is consistent with pankration's emphasis on freely applying grappling in conjunction with striking techniques whenever possible.

V/UPRIGHT GRAPPLING SKILLS
(Orthia Pale)

Also essential to the pankratiast in standup fighting is grappling, which includes gripping, clinching, and taking one's adversary off his feet. Grappling is perhaps the earliest systematized combat form. It was refined in ancient Greece, where wrestling was first introduced into the Olympic games of 708 B.C. The Roman Empire embraced wrestling with the same passion as the Greeks had, and developed one of the main wrestling styles still used today, the *Greco-Roman*. They adapted the sport to their own traditions and refined it even further, barring some of its more brutal features.

Grappling supplies the advantage to the "total" martial artist. Proficient grapplers have proven time after time that they can tie up and immobilize even the best punchers and kickers. Any martial art which does not include grappling and ground-fighting skills in its repertoire is not adequately preparing its followers for actual combat. There is a major difference, however, between wrestling and submission grappling. The first is a sport with the ultimate goal of pinning one's shoulders to the mat. The object of the latter is to force the opponent to quit or else suffer dislocation, even death.

Although grappling techniques are most often applied from close range or from a clinch, they can also be initiated from longer distances by feinting to bridge the gap, or as a follow-up to a strike or kick. Grappling can also be effectively employed from this distance by drawing the opponent into leading, then using a grappling tool as a countering move. The modern pankratiast is trained to apply his knowledge of grappling from any range presented in a combat situation.

The modern pankratiast does not rely purely on strength when grappling, but on proper technique and sensitivity to his opponent's movements. In addition, he thrives on exploiting the rival fighter's weaknesses and mistakes. He is well aware that once on the ground, his foe will inevitably make a wrong move and once that happens, he will instantly take advantage of it.

Grappling, though extremely effective, demands extraordinary stamina and a great sense of leverage. Physical conditioning is imperative to effective grappling. Every muscle of the human body is utilized to the fullest degree. It requires the utmost balance, quickness, cardiovascular endurance, mental toughness, and kinesthetic awareness to control a larger opponent or to reverse a seemingly hopeless position to one of advantage. An essential factor in grappling is knowing where one's body is in relation to his adversary. By establishing a solid base, a skillful grappler can turn his foe's energy against him, thus conserving his own energy.

CLOSING THE GAP AND CLINCHING

Transitioning from striking range to close-quarter grappling requires that the pankratiast charge the opponent at top speed and without warning. Any hesitation in the maneuver will most likely cause the opponent to avoid the attack or counter as you "shoot" in low. It is important, in closing the gap, that the grappler not absorb a solid blow on the way in. Sometimes, a preliminary hand feint or low kick is used to distract the opponent's attention away from his lower body being targeted for the assault. Another effective maneuver is to first disrupt the opponent's balance with a powerful low round kick to the legs. If the opposing fighter can be spun around, the pankratiast will take immediate advantage of this vulnerable situation to flank him from behind. Attacking one's foe from the rear flank is a most advantageous position to be in for maximum grappling effectiveness. An opposing fighter must be careful not to expose his back to a trained pankratiast.

The Shoot

Once the pankratiast has closed the distance, he will apply a "clinch", gripping the opponent about the waist, legs, neck, or some other part of the body in preparation of taking the fight to the ground. This is sometimes referred to as the *tie-up* position.

The Clinch (tie-up)

TAKEDOWNS

A takedown is a means of knocking the opponent off his feet and placing him in a vulnerable position on the ground whereby a follow-up offensive, either a strike or another grappling action, is normally used. The basic takedowns utilized in mu tau pankration are the leg tackle, the waist lock, foot sweeps, and throws.

Leg Tackle

The **leg tackle** is a takedown in which either one or both legs are grasped. The double-leg takedown is more effective whereas the opposing fighter has both legs under him, while attacking one leg requires more effort to bring the opposing fighter's body down to the ground. The single leg tackle, on the other hand, is normally executed against a kicking offensive, when one's balance is centered on but one leg.

Double-leg tackle

The pankratiast lowers the center of gravity in his stance while maintaining good balance and then shoots in, securing his head on either side of the opponent's hips. Gripping the opponent's legs at either knee height or the thighs, he drives his upper body into the opponent's midsection or upper leg area. The simultaneous action of scooping the legs while exerting pressure against the midsection results in an effective takedown. This technique can also be applied from behind the opponent. From this position, the ankles would be gripped and the shoulder exerting pressure against the upper leg area.

Single leg takedown

Waistlocks

Another common takedown technique of the pankratiast is the **waistlock** wherein the opponent is gripped about the belt line from either the front or behind, and then maneuvered to the ground where he can be finished off. The legs are often used in this technique to further break down the opposing fighter's balance. The pankratiast wraps one of his legs around the opponent's leg at the knee or calf area while forcing him down. The heel often kicks sharply into the calf. The hands are wrapped about the midsection with the fingers interlocked behind the back. A variation of this technique is the reverse waistlock. This involves wrapping the arms about the opponent's back and interlocking the fingers in front of him. This technique is often employed to counter a leg tackle.

Front waistlock.

Front waistlock with trip.

Rear waistlock.

Reverse Waistlocks

Foot Sweeps

Also effective in taking a man down is **sweeping** the leg or legs from under him. Sweeps are effective after a fighter's leg has first been seized or grabbed in a kicking assault. A slowly-executed kick or any kicking attack to the midsection or higher is vulnerable to being seized by a good grappling technician. Once the leg is caught, a sweep to the supporting leg at the kneejoint will follow with the intent of toppling a fighter.

1. Seize opponent's kick.   2. Sweep the supporting leg at the ankle.

Throws

Throws are also employed in MTP to take the opponent to the ground. One such throwing technique is the **hip and headlock throw**. After securing a clinch from infighting range, an opponent is often downed by grabbing him around the head while flipping him over the hip. This enables the pankratiast to maintain control of the opponent's head when the fight hits the ground.

The **shoulder throw** is an upper body takedown in which the pankratiast locks an arm by means of an underhook and flips his adversary over his shoulder. This is accomplished with a quick pivoting movement of the feet and a forward dip at the waist. The adversary's arm is controlled at all times throughout the maneuver so that an arm lock can be applied when the fight goes to the ground.

Another throw which also serves to finish one's foe is the **suplex**, a maneuver in which the grappler executes a waist lock, gripping his opponent around the beltline from either the front (belly to belly) or behind (belly to back). He then falls backward while shooting the opposing combatant over his shoulder and into the ground. The objective is to not only throw the opponent but to crunch his head and shoulders from the resulting ground impact. This technique is a dangerous one, as it could cause a broken neck if properly executed.

Front Suplex (Belly-to-Belly)

Rear Suplex (Belly-to-Back)

BASIC DEFENSES AGAINST TAKEDOWNS

The Sprawl

Other than attempting to catch the offensive grappler on the way in with an uppercut or knee strike, the basic defense of the pankratiast against leg takedowns or tackles is the **sprawl**. As the opponent initiates a tackling maneuver, this technique is executed by moving the hips out and away from the attacker's grasp by kicking one's legs straight back. The opponent's torso is then controlled by grasping his head or upper extremities. The opponent's body can then be shoved downward and underneath into a precarious position.

The pankration practitioner could then spin onto his rival's back into the top control position and unleash a more aggressive offensive.

SPRAWL EXECUTION

1. Ready Positions.

2. Opponent shoots for legs.

3. Kick legs back and drop weight downward on opponent.

4. Neutralize opponent's movement on the ground.

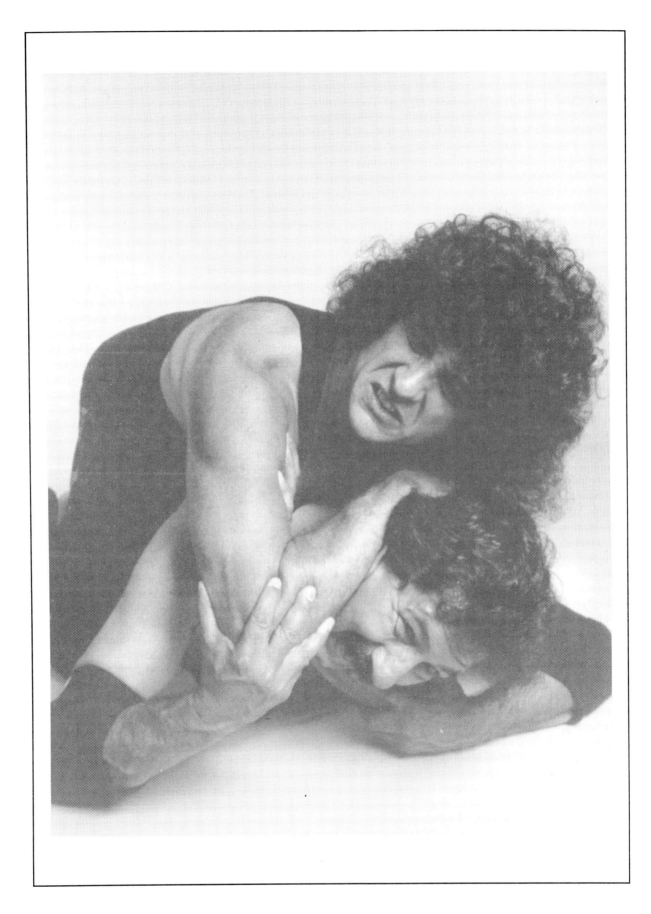

VI/GROUND-FIGHTING SKILLS
(Kato Pankration)

Ground-fighting is an essential element of pankration. It includes proper maneuvering, both offensive skills of striking and grappling, and sound defensive tactics. With a single-minded focus of attaining victory through any means possible, pankratiasts are trained to end a fight in a matter of seconds, yet are prepared to do battle for lengthy periods of time, if need be, to win. In most cases, they will end the confrontation at ground level with either a relentless series of blows or a submission grappling technique.

Although a pankratiast is capable of ending a fight in an upright posture with a knockout blow, there is at least an equal emphasis on going to the ground where submission grappling skills are combined with finishing strikes to defeat the opponent. This is especially the case when the fighters are standing toe-to-toe and too close for the striking tools to be effective. In this comprehensive art, the key is to be ready for any type of opponent and to fit in to any form of combative environment that might arise. Whereas street fights frequently end up on the ground, mu tau, in the tradition of pankration, prepares its fighters for every possible situation.

In practice sparring, once an opponent is taken down, the action continues on the ground with each fighter attempting to force the other into surrendering verbally or by "tapping out" (i.e. slapping the mat twice). In an all-out fight, the ultimate intention of the pankratiast is to render the opponent either helpless or senseless.

There are two basic offensive skills in kato pankration: submission grappling holds and finishing strikes. Of course, before one can successfully apply these skills, he must be able to make the transition from the outside range to infighting, and from a standing posture to the ground. Once on the ground, he must gain a position of control over his opponent. The grappling skills of mu tau pankration are influenced by both Greco-Roman and freestyle wrestling, and combat judo.

GROUND CONTROL

Once the fight goes to the ground, the pankratiast attempts to obtain the best tactical position for subduing his opponent while smothering his ability to strike back effectively. A superb example of this is the *top control position*, often referred to as the "mount" in other systems of self-defense that specialize in groundfighting. This maneuver often follows a takedown or knockdown from a strike with the pankratiast working his way on top of the opponent and straddling his waist, locking his legs under his rival's upper thighs. In modern sport wrestling, this is similar to "riding" the back of one's opponent.

The top control position offers excellent placement for controlling the opponent's movements, and launching an effective assault. If the opponent is facing upward, the mounter can pummel his opponent, reigning downward punches and elbow strikes to the face. If he attempts to roll to the side to avoid the blows, the pankratiast will respond by turning him onto his stomach and applying either a deadly choke or arm lock. Needless to say, this tactical ploy of pinning one's opponent is extremely difficult to escape from if it is properly executed and maintained.

Top control position (side view).

Top control (back view).

The top position is an enviable place for the grappler. With the opponent face down on the ground, the man on top will use his legs and his full weight to pin his foe so he cannot execute a "roll-out" maneuver, or escape. From here, the most obvious follow-up move is a rear stranglehold. If the opponent resists, an effective tactic would be to yank his head back by pulling the hair and then applying the finishing grip about the throat.

For the fighter who is pinned on the bottom, this is one of the worst situations to be in. Due to the relative position of the shoulders and face, the fighter on top can easily strike the face of his opponent, but this is not possible for the man on the bottom. In short; it is easier to strike downward than it is upward in this situation. In addition, the combatant who has the top position has the advantage of leverage to gain more punching room and deliver more force behind their blows. The fighter pinned underneath cannot fully cock their arm since its motion is restricted by the ground.

Also effective for the top fighter is side control. While this position does not allow instant offense, it offers the advantage of controlling the opponent on the bottom, and strategically moving into the top mounted position where a more efficient attack can be made.

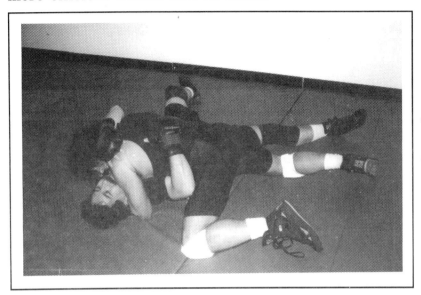

Side control.

Knee-in-chest.

A variation to the side control position is to place the knee into the chest of the opponent. The use of the knee in this manner adds leverage for follow-up strikes or submission locks while neutralizing the opponent against the ground.

FINISHING HOLDS

JOINT LOCKS

Locks applied to an opponent's limbs have long been characteristic of pankration's grappling arsenal. Opportunities for applying joint locks are more frequent when one or both combatants are on the ground. Joint locks have but one purpose -- to force the opponent to quit or else suffer dislocation or a broken limb. The joints that are most often attacked are the fingers, the wrist, the elbow, the shoulder, the knee, and the ankle. The key is to twist or bend the limb against the joint to a point where the pain is unbearable for the opposing fighter. There are a number of variations of arm and leg locks employed in MTP. The following are but a sampling of the major techniques.

Arm Bar

One of the most common arm locks is the arm bar. Although the technique is applicable from a standing position, it is most often employed when on the ground. The arm bar can be used in a variety of ways, and frequently follows the top mounted position with the fighter on the bottom facing up.

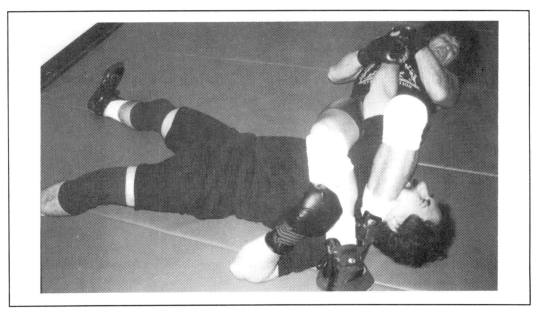

To apply the arm bar while standing, the same basic principles are followed. The pankratiast grips the arm by the wrist while kneeling on the opposing fighter's head. He then leans his upper body backward with the elbow braced against the crotch area.

Standing arm bar.

The arm bar can also be applied from a kneeling position with the opposing fighter on his back. The right hand stabilizes the shoulder while the left arm wraps under the elbow. Force is exerted by pushing down on the shoulder while lifting up on the elbow joint.

Kneeling arm bar.

EXECUTING THE SIDE ARM BAR FROM TOP CONTROL

This is an excellent maneuver in which the mounted fighter swings to his left while gaining control of his opponent's arm. He then grips the arm by the wrist with both hands, holding it against the lower stomach area. In completing the move, the pankratiast then lies back, locking his legs over the neck and chest of the opponent to prevent him from rolling out. To exert pressure on the elbow joint, the pelvic region is elevated while pulling the arm downward.

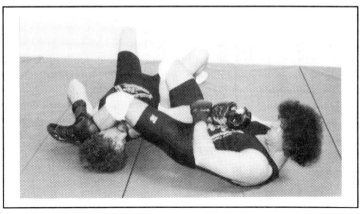

Hammer Lock

The hammer lock is another effective finishing arm hold. In using this technique, the pankratiast employs both hands to fold the opponent's arm behind his back by gripping the elbow and wrist. Pressure is applied by yanking the trapped arm upward. The hammer lock can be applied with your back on the ground, or from the top control position.

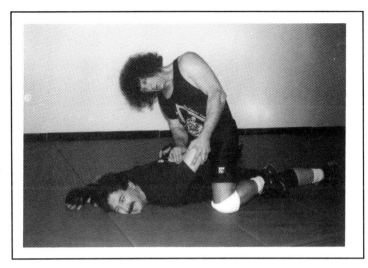

Hammerlock from top control position.

Hammerlock from bottom position.

Hammerlock on ground.

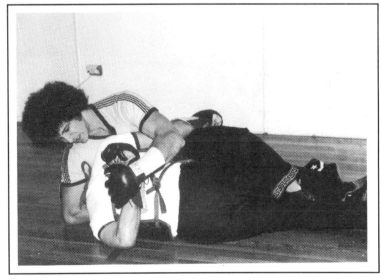

Elbow Break

The elbow break is executed from either a kneeling or standing posture. It is considered a "sacrifice" maneuver as it requires that your back be turned to the opponent. The positioning of the opponent's arm is also critical. It must have the palm facing upward. Having grasped the wrist or lower forearm with both hands, the opponent's elbow is placed over the shoulder and then forcefully yanked downward. The resulting action will easily break the arm at the elbow joint. Due to the risk in turning one's back, however, this technique must be applied swiftly and without deliberation.

Leg Scissors Arm Lock

The leg scissors arm lock is executed from the bottom position as the top mounted fighter is attempting to gain the position of advantage. In this hold, the opponent's arm is pinned against the chest, while the legs wrap about the shoulder of the trapped arm. The hips are raised to apply pressure.

Ankle Lock

In applying the ankle lock, the pankratiast simply grasps his opponent's lower leg at the ankle and twists it forcefully to either side. This technique is applicable either when upright or during ground fighting.

Standing ankle lock.

Ankle lock on ground.

Step-Over Toe Hold

A slight variation of the ankle lock is the **step-over toe hold**. The pankratiast executes this submission technique by twisting the downed fighter's ankle as he quickly steps over his leg.

Double Leg Lock

With the opponent on the ground and facing upward, the **double leg lock** is an effective submission technique. It involves applying pressure by first lifting up on both of the opponent's legs. He is then rolled over and straddled by the pankratiast, who lifts up on his legs while leaning back. Not only does this cause extreme leg pain but can serve as a back-breaker as well.

Inward Leg Wind

From a sitting position on the ground, the **leg wind** is a painful submission lock whereby the pankratiast positions his own leg against the opponent's inner knee area, grips the lower leg at the ankle, and then applies pressure by forcing the trapped leg against his own knee.

SUBMISSION CHOKEHOLDS

Choking techniques have always been popular grappling tactics since pankration's earliest beginnings, with strangulation being the most frequent cause of fatalities in matches. Arm chokes are the most popular, although the hands and even the legs can be applied. Once a firm grip has been secured about an opponent's throat, he will immediately submit before any further harm can be administered to him.

Strangleholds can easily cause one's victim to lose consciousness by preventing the flow of oxygenated blood to the brain. This is done by either compressing the carotid arteries from either side of the neck, or by forcing pressure on the trachea or windpipe in front of the neck, from the Adam's Apple to the top of the sternum.

Mu tau pankration training emphasizes the development of strong neck muscles to resist the damaging effects of a chokehold. A choke, however, is potentially lethal and difficult to escape from. Although it can be administered from a variety of positions, the choke is most commonly applied from the top control position.

Front Stranglehold

There are numerous chokes used by trained pankratiasts. One example is the front stranglehold, otherwise known as the "guillotine choke." This technique can be applied either from a standing position or prone.

Rear Choke

The most lethal stranglehold in mu tau pankration is the rear choke, in which the opponent's back is to you and you have throttled his neck with both forearms, one about the windpipe and the other exerting force against the back of the neck. This submission technique is primarily applied from the top control position with the opposing fighter face down.

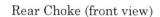
Rear Choke (front view)

Rear Choke (side view)

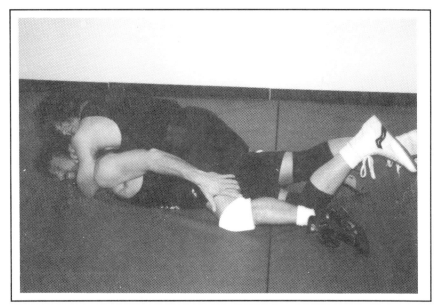

Klimakismos

The **klimakismos** (Greek: ladder trick) is a combination rear choke and body scissors which is often initiated from an upright position and eventually ends up on the ground. In this technique, the pankratiast springs upon his adversary's back after either nudging him off-balance with a leg kick or attaining the rear flank angle on him. This is an ancient finishing move and is well-documented in the early days of the sport's inclusion in the Greek Olympiad.

Klimakismos on ground.

Side Choke

This submission stranglehold is applied from the side, with the body perpendicular to that of the opponent who is on his back. The technique resembles a headlock but with one major difference; the opposing fighter's arm is pushed across the front of his neck. While one arm encircles the back of the neck, the top pankratiast tucks his head alongside the shoulder of the trapped arm. Both hands interlock causing pressure to the other side of the neck. Using one's body weight to push downward on the trapped arm adds to the effectiveness of the choke.

Cross-Arm and Single-Hand Chokes

Other choking tools available to the pankratiast include the front cross-arm choke and the single-hand choke. To be effective, the cross-arm choke should only be applied on an opponent who is wearing a shirt. In this way, the clothing is utilized by the pankratiast to maintain a tight grip upon the throat. The hands are crossed and pressure exerted downward upon both sides of the neck.

The cross-arm choke.

The single-hand choke, on the other hand, is employed from a variety of positions both standing and on the ground. It involves the use of one hand to clutch and squeeze the windpipe.

Single hand choke.

Leg Strangles

The legs are also used in applying submission chokes. Again, this technique is most frequently employed with either one or both combatants on the ground. It is a useful countering move against an opponent who is attempting to pass the guard. As the fighter on top tries to pass, the bottom man will scissors his legs around his head, attempting to place the inside of the knee of one leg over the ankle of his other leg. One of the opponent's arms is also grasped with both hands to prevent an escape from the leg choke. Additional pressure is possible by releasing the arm, grabbing the back of the head and pulling it forward while squeezing the thighs about the neck. The pressure exerted by the opponent's upper arm and your thigh will diminish the supply of blood to his brain, rendering him unconscious.

Leg strangle against crouching opponent.

Leg strangle against opponent on ground.

OTHER FINISHING TECHNIQUES

GROUND STRIKES

On the ground, pankration fighters are proficient in pummeling their opponent into submission from the top or side control positions. Whether the opponent is facing up or has his back turned, the practitioner will punch or elbow his foe to the head, face or neck to subdue him. He will also use his knees to drop upon his adversary's body or head. If the pankratiast is on the bottom, he will utilize his feet to kick the opponent in any open target. Ground strikes are effective in weakening the opponent in preparation for assuming a more advantageous position for subduing him and are used in conjunction with grappling holds.

When punching from the mount, a pankratiast will often pin his opponent with his free hand. This prohibits the bottom man from elevating forward to try and grab the combatant on top and allows more room for the mounted fighter to deliver his strikes. The free hand can also employed to trap or immobilize the opponent's arms so that he cannot block the blows.

Elbow strike to face.

Downward elbow strike to neck.

Punching from back mount.

Body punching from
top control.

Knee drop to face.

HEAD & NECK MANIPULATIONS

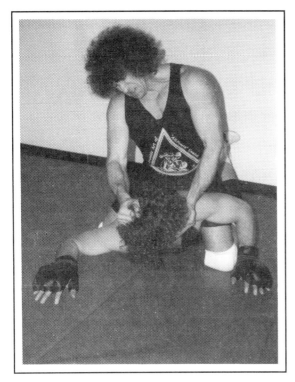

Once the pankratiast has secured the top control position, he can also apply other submission grips about the head and neck areas other than a choke. A simple **neck crank** can be used, whereby the opponent's head is twisted violently to either the left or right by grabbing his hair and chin.

Another effective alternative is the **chin lock**, an immobilizing hold in which the pankratiast employs both hands to grip the chin of one's adversary and force the head back while sitting on his back. Either of these techniques is potentially disabling.

BASIC GROUND-FIGHTING DEFENSES

In defending from the bottom position on the ground, the mu tau pankratiast often finds himself on his back. In grappling-oriented styles such as Japanese and Brazilian jujutsu, shoot-fighting, and pancrase, the term **guard** refers to a defensive ploy used against the top mounted position. This form of ground defense can be applied from either in close or long range.

Before the opponent can firmly position himself in a fully-mounted position, the bottom fighter attempts to keep the top man between his legs. He then scissors his legs about his waist, making it difficult for his opponent to gain the needed leverage to advance and effectively control him. A skilled groundfighter will also pull his opponent's head close to his chest, thereby nullifying his ability to launch an effective punch.

Guard defense from bottom position.

In defending from the bottom position, pankratiasts can assume control over their adversary and ultimately defeat him by executing an arm lock or choke while in this supine posture. If the top man attempts to stand and launch downward punches to the face, the fighter on the bottom can use his feet to stop the blows by striking his biceps. This positioning also offers the choice of playing a waiting game to conserve one's own energy while wearing down his opponent. He will then take the offensive once exhaustion has forced a mistake from the opposing combatant.

Foot block from the bottom position.

HEEL KICKS FROM THE BOTTOM POSITION

In a long range situation where the pankratiast is on his back against a standing fighter who is attempting to move in, the feet become important tools. They can be employed to deliver front, side, and round kicks to the legs, body, or even the face of the aggressor. These techniques are not only used to hurt the opposition but to secure a more advantageous strategic position from which to attack.

Side kick to knee.

Heel to groin.

116

Heel kick to face.

The Elevator

The **elevator** is a basic defensive move used against a top mounted fighter. The pankratiast, from the bottom position, simply performs a back bridge by elevating his hips using his head and legs. The objective of this technique is to jolt the opponent upward, thereby disrupting his balance and weight so that the bottom fighter can gain better position from which to defend himself.

Foul Tactics: Techniques for Release

In the street, "foul" tactics are utilized in conjunction with grappling techniques to enhance the effectiveness of a hold or to escape from a submission maneuver. Included in these tactics are ear and hairpulling for exerting control over one's adversary, and biting and eye-gouging to gain release from the opponent's grip. To escape a rear choke, for example, pankratiasts often pin the chin against the top of the breastbone and use their hand to block the grip against the throat. They then grasp for the fingers and bend them back forcefully. In gouging the opponent's eyes, either the thumb or the extended fingertips are used.

FOUL TACTICS

Hairpulling.

Fingerbending.

Earpulling.

EYE GOUGING FROM THE GROUND

Thumb strike.

Finger jab.

Biting.

VII/COMBAT STRATEGY

Fighting is often thought of as one combatant simply overpowering the other. In reality, the winner in battle is not necessarily the stronger individual. Victory is often achieved by the fighter with better technique and strategy. It is a fact that a smaller man can overcome one who relies totally on physical attributes alone. He who can out-think his opponent always has the advantage.

Strategy is of paramount importance to the modern pankratiast. Applying one's offensive skills in a sound, tactical manner is considered the highest level of proficiency in the art, one requiring superb technique as well as exceptional mental aptitude. These tactics include set-ups, combinations, and countering.

SETUPS

A set-up is a means of disrupting an opponent's timing while simultaneously inducing a defensive reaction, thereby creating an opening for one's attack. Setups are based on the effective use of feinting.

Feinting is based on the element of surprise, utilizing some form of body or limb movement to deceive the adversary. They use cunning and technical deception to provide a false impression of your intended action. Then, as your opponent's predicted response is made, your attack finds the opening in his defense. When fused with direct attacks and combinations, the opponent is constantly baffled as to what is real and what is not.

The feint is a partially-committed blow or kick that appears to be the start of a sound offensive tactic, but is really intended to elicit a defensive reaction from the opposing fighter. His reaction then creates an opening for another type of attack.

High hand feint induces high block.

Feinting only sets up momentary openings. To score effectively upon these exposed targets necessitates instant reflex action as well as a foreknowledge of what openings will be created by certain feints. Such familiarity demands practice, for only through the actual use of many feints against many different types of fighters may a general reaction tendency be determined.

A feint cannot look like a feint; it must appear to be an actual attack. The only way to deliver a successful indirect offensive is to be able to feint convincingly, and thus obtain the maximum reaction from your opponent. If your foe does not respond accordingly, your feinting is not being properly executed. When feinting, be fully aware of your opponent and his reaction. He must react in such a way that he actually feels threatened by that preparatory move.

Low hand feint induces low block.

Low kick feint induces low block.

Probably the most difficult part in applying a feint is in the perfection of one's sense of timing. The execution must allow for a slight pause to enable the opponent to react prior to the delivery of the actual attack. It must be done in such a manner that is unable to determine what technique is on its way. Repetitious drilling on this pause is crucial in order to apply the feint effectively.

The initial movement must permit you to gain critical distance between yourself and the opposition. This preparatory maneuver will throw off your rival's timing as you follow up with the intended technique.

SOME BASIC SET-UPS:

- **Low Jab Feint to High Lead Hook.** From the ready poses, induce your opponent to lower his hands by faking a jab to the body. Once an opening in the high line presents itself, deliver a solid lead hook to the jaw.

- **Jab Feint to Double Leg Tackle.**

  This is an example of a high distraction setting up a low attack, in this case, a grappling takedown.

- **High Jab Feint to Low Back Leg Kick.**

  From readiness, force the opponent to raise his guard with a feint jab to the face. Once he adjusts his defense, step in with a back-leg round kick to the thigh.

COMBINATIONS

Mu tau pankratiasts are well-schooled in delivering their offensive tools in combination. A combination is best described as two or more attack techniques delivered in fluid succession. The attacks flow from one into another naturally, the objective being to overwhelm the opponent with a flurry of moves without giving him time to react effectively. For example, it is difficult to score, with a single blow, against a fighter with a good, air-tight defense. By combining successive techniques into a natural sequence, a heavier burden is placed on one's defense. Well-planned and executed combinations get through even the tightest guard.

In standup fighting, one blow may not stop an opponent, but an accumulation of strikes will often do the job. In MTP, combinations can consist of a series of striking techniques, grappling maneuvers, or a blending of strikes with grappling. Most of the striking combinations employ the hands. These punching combinations are cleverly-orchestrated sequences, with each opening creating another. In all cases, each blow or movement in the sequence is intended to land or uncover gaps in one's defense for follow-up attacks. This method of taking the offensive requires economical motion, tight and alert defensive covering, speed and surprise, and confidence in execution. To develop effective combinations, one begins by perfecting a series of basic moves that easily follow each other. The initial technique of a combination is normally the most important as it sets up your opponent. If the first blow dazes him or causes him to drop his guard, the follow-up strikes are certain to land cleanly and hurt him.

The first technique must always be executed explosively and with excellent timing in order to catch the opposing fighter in a moment of weakness. This might be as he is altering his guard, if he loses concentration for an instant, or if he has been distracted by a false movement. It is also essential to begin combinations with a lead jab, since it is the closer to the targets and easier to land.

Whereas speed and nontelegraphic motion are crucial factors in successfully landing combinations, the next blow should begin without delay as the prior one is being retracted. Distancing is also of paramount importance when attempting combination strikes. Each technique in the series should be able to make contact with the adversary by either taking a slight step forward or back. Beginning a combo from too far out will only allow your opponent greater time to counter or catch you with a shot while you are in the process of stringing your blows together.

Striking Combinations

There are literally hundreds of striking combinations in MTP. The following is but a sampling of some of the major ones. In most sequences, the combination is initiated with the lead jab which serves to set up the heavier blows of the series.

- **Jab/Reverse Thrust**

- **Lead Uppercut/Rear Elbow Strike (infighting).**

- **Jab/Lead Hook.**

1. Ready Positions.

2. Close gap with jab to face.

3. Pivot hips for leverage.

4. Lead hook punch to head.

• Jab/Rear Thrust/Lead Hook.

1. Ready positions.

2. Close the gap with a jab.

3. Deliver rear thrust to face.

4. Finish combination with lead hook to head.

- **Jab/Low Lead Hook/High Lead Hook.**

- **Jab/Rear Thrust/Neck Grab to Knee.**

Strikes to Takedowns

Sometimes a transition to grappling range is set up by a striking technique. The following are some basic examples.

- **Low Front Kick to Waistlock.**
  In this series, the takedown follows a front thrust kick to the knee.

- **Leg Kick to Rear Waistlock Takedown.** From readiness, take the offensive with a low kick to the legs. With the opponent spun off-balance from the impact of the kick, close with a rear waistlock. Wrap one leg around his legs and force him face-forward to the ground.

Takedowns to Follow-Up Submissions

Grappling combinations usually consist of a takedown or throw followed by a submission hold or finishing strikes. Once the fight goes to the ground, one must be skilled in continuing the relentless attack.

- **Front Waist Tackle to Top Mount to Finishing Strikes/Choke.**

Once you gain a waistlock clinch and take the fight to the ground, maneuver into the top control position and unleash repeated punches to the face. If the opponent turns to avoid the strikes, flip him onto his stomach and apply a rear choke.

- **Shoulder Throw to Side Arm Lock on ground.**

  Using an arm throw to topple the opponent, continue to hold onto his arm, applying a submission arm bar from the side once you are on the ground.

- **Rear Leg Tackle to Leg Lock.** Close the gap by shooting for the legs and quickly spin to the rear flank position. Grip the opponent's legs at the lower shins and drive him face forward into the ground by pushing against the back of his knees with your shoulders. Once he is down, maneuver on top of his legs and apply an inward leg wind to force him to submit.

- **Strike to Throw to Submission Choke.** In this series, a strike is used to close the gap for a takedown and follow-up finishing hold. After delivering an eye jab, move in with a hip/headlock throw. Once on the ground, roll the opponent's shoulder in front of his face and interlock the fingers under the side of his neck. Apply a side choke by leveraging your weight in pushing the head against the shoulder and squeezing with the arms against the other side of his neck.

 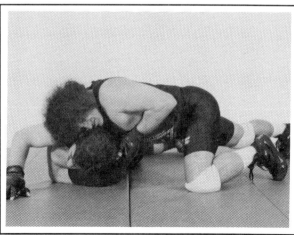

COUNTER-ATTACK

A counter-attack is a retaliatory blow or grappling action given in reply to an opponent's lead. It is not purely a defensive tactic but is a means of taking the offensive once the opponent's attack has first been thwarted. Counters are broken down into two areas: counter-strikes and counter-grappling. In grappling, when a takedown or submission maneuver is countered, it is often referred to as a *reversal*.

Counter-Strikes

There are three elements essential to effective counterstriking: the opponent's lead, the method of avoiding the lead, and the retaliation itself. Against punches, for example, a blow with the forward hand exposes the frontal part of the body, while a rear-side blow exposes all of the upper trunk.

In avoiding leads, a fighter must decide instantaneously whether to parry, block, apply an evasive move, or attempt to beat the opponent to the attack. Parrying leaves but one hand to counter but has the advantage in mu tau pankration of being utilized concurrently as a trap to inhibit the opponent's continued use of that arm. Evasions such as slipping and ducking allow two-fisted counters.

An effective counter sometimes depends on **drawing**, or luring the opposing fighter into leading. By offering him what appears to be an opening, you force the opponent into "taking the bait." Though it is a deliberate error, it must never appear this way to him as an experienced fighter will seldom, if ever, fall prey to a "setup."

Drawing the attack is a premeditated action and its success depends upon enticing your rival into attacking at the openings being presented. Examples of drawing include lowering the rear hand guard to expose the head, lowering the lead hand for head exposure, and holding the guard extremely high to invite a body attack.

SOME BASIC COUNTER-STRIKING TACTICS:

- **Front Shin Block to Back-Leg Round Kick to thigh.** In this counter, the fighter on the left attacks with a leg kick which is blocked with the shin. The defender quickly retaliates with a back-leg round kick to the thigh.

- Slip Jab to Side Kick to knee.

- Block Hook to Two Elbow Strikes to head.

Reversals (Counter-Grappling)

A reversal is a grappling maneuver used to alter the control situation in a fight. It is actually a counter to a takedown attempt, strategic position, or a hold.

Reversals require an excellent sense of leverage. Once the fighter feels a shift in balance such that the opponent's weight is distributed in one direction, he will "roll" in that direction to gain a better position. This same principle also applies to applying holds. The key is to go **with** the direction of the exerted force, not against it.

Most reversals in MTP are employed against either a top mounted fighter or one who has attempted a throw or takedown maneuver. The following are some basic examples of countering with grappling and reversing the control factor.

- **Forward Roll to Mount to Choke.** From readiness, pankratiast on left dodges and parries a lunging straight lead, and applies a rear waistllock. The lock is reversed by grabbing the opponent's hands, tucking your chin down and rolling forward. Complete the maneuver by obtaining top control and finish the opponent by choking him out, using the opponent's own shoulder to exert pressure against his throat.

- **Trapped-Arm Roll (Choke Escape) to Arm Lock**. While on your knees against a mounted opponent who is attempting a rear choke, pin your chin against your breastbone. Then trap the opponent's arm while doing a side roll. Maintain your grip on his arm and apply pressure against the elbow joint.

- **Arm-Throw Counter to Klimakismos.**

From a clinch, the opponent attempts an arm throw. Maneuver onto his back while using your free hand to push against his lower back. This will interrupt his momentum in throwing you. Then take him to the ground with a rear stranglehold while applying a leg scissors about his waist.

- **Sprawl to Top Control to Choke.**

Against a leg takedown attempt, execute a sprawl by kicking the legs back and dropping your weight on top of the opponent. Quickly spin to the right and obtain the top control position. Snake the left arm underneath the opponent's throat and end the conflict with a rear choke.

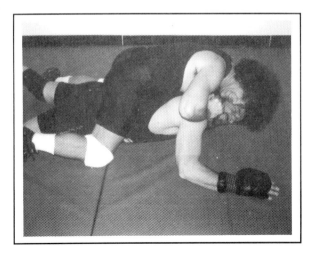

- **Counter headlock/hip throw with Belly-to-Back Suplex.** Against the opponent who charges in grabbing you about the head in preparation for a hip throw, maneuver behind him and clinch him around his waist. Throw him backwards with a suplex. In this countering move, your stomach should be making contact with his back.

- **Counter waistlock with front Suplex to top control to strikes.**

  Against an opponent who shoots for a front waistlock, grab him about the neck in a guillotine choke and then quickly roll back throwing him to the ground. As he lands on his back, roll on top of him, pin him by using the left hand on his throat to nullify his movement, and unleash strikes.

150

- **Counter shoot with choke from top mount.** Against a shoot for the legs, sprawl the opponent and spin to your left into a top mount. Deliver punches to the body and head to weaken him. Finish with a rear choke.

- **Counter kick with sweep to leg lock to strikes.** Against a kick, seize the leg and sweep the supporting foot at the calf. Maintain the grip on the foot and pull back on it. The knee is wedged behind the back of the opponent's knee. Deliver finishing elbow strikes to the head.

VIII/SPARTAN DISCIPLINE

An important aspect in the study of pankration is a traditional Greek code of conduct referred to as *Spartan discipline*. This discipline, inspired by the ancient inhabitants of Sparta, was observed by all warriors and athletes. It was necessary in preparing the mind and body to successfully cope with the demands of life-or-death combat in the arena or on the battlefield. Today, MTP imparts Spartan discipline to its followers, applying it to both no-holds-barred combat in the street as well as the continual striving for perfection of one's craft. According to the ancient Greeks, the mental and physical aspects of an athlete are inseparable; one cannot exist or function without the other. To prepare for combat requires that the mu tau pankratiast aspire to be a highly-conditioned athlete, and to experience realistic simulations of combat in his training.

CONDITIONING EXERCISES

Sheer physical fitness is a significant part of the martial arts but a rigorous conditioning program is often neglected in the constant striving of perfecting the combat techniques themselves. To a pankratiast, perfecting the tools is certainly essential, but so is maintaining or upgrading one's physical condition. Actually, both are necessary to be successful in realistic fighting. If there are truly any "secrets" to acquiring martial arts proficiency, then it is hard training. Proper training is a means of disciplining the mind and building the body. It involves sufficient rest, good nutrition, and plenty of exercise. One will discover that his kicks, strikes, grappling skills, and staying-power will attain peak efficiency if he is fit.

A martial artist must be aware of those exercises that benefit his skills and others which might hinder his progress. Lifting extremely heavy weights, for instance, is not advised as this might be detrimental to both speed and flexibility, vital attributes of a trained pankratiast. The exercises emphasized in MTP can roughly be divided into three groups: those which are designed to loosen and limber the body; those designed to supply endurance to the muscular and cardiovascular systems of the body; and those which enhance muscular strength.

Warmups

Athletes always warm up before a game or contest. They are well aware that to perform well, they must prepare their bodies to undergo rigorous physical activity. Any form of strenuous exercise that taxes one's muscles, tendons, ligaments, heart, and lungs should be preceded by well-planned warm-up exercises and followed by similar cooling-down exercises.

Because it is a vigorous form of exercise, any full-contact combative art places stress on the human body. In order to withstand such stress, muscles must be made loose and supple, and blood must start pumping at an exercise level. Large amounts of oxygen must be taken into the body and carried by the bloodstream throughout the system.

In a comparable fashion, one must be careful to taper off his exercise, not come to an abrupt halt. Runners usually jog a slow lap, swimmers take a last swim. This is the cool-down phase, a critical link between rigorous activity and relative calm.

An average warmup period might last approximately ten to fifteen minutes but this varies according to the climate that one lives in. Mu tau training features a small group of simple warmup exercises which are effective in stepping up circulation, limbering certain muscles, improving mobility, and readying the body for the rugged demands of the training regimen to follow. An MTP trainee avoids rushing through this warmup phase as many athletes sometimes do. He will work through them thoroughly to gain the most beneficial results.

The warmups performed in modern pankration training include *neck rolls* which are designed to loosen the neck muscles. The head is rotated fully in both directions, gently at the start with a gradual increase in range of motion and forcefulness. *Trunk twisting* stretches the lateral muscles of the midsection (obliques) and loosens the muscles of the chest and shoulders. An empty bar is held across the shoulders in this exercise to enhance the ballistic whipping action at the waist.

neck rolls

trunk twisting

cat-stretch

A good warmup for limbering the lower back and hips is the *cat-stretch*, basically a pushup movement where you slide the body along the floor as far as possible before arching your back at the completion.

Other warmups include *trunk bends*. By bending the upper body as far back as possible, the lower back muscles are loosened. Bending forward from the waist and grasping the ankles while touching one's head to his knees stretches the rear thigh muscles.

rear trunk bends

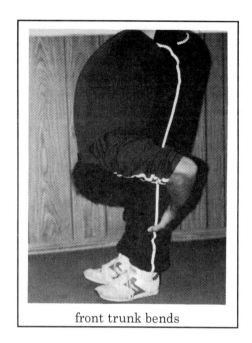

front trunk bends

Leg stretching exercises are also part of warming up. All athletic endeavors requiring heavy use of the legs incorporate stretching exercises into their conditioning programs in order to prevent pulled muscles and tendons and for greater flexibility.

Research has proven that regular stretching can bring about improvements in flexibility, accuracy, speed of movement, agility, and balance. Just as important, stretching increases tissue elasticity, thereby decreasing the likelihood of injury. Strained muscles impede movement, but more importantly, it means torn muscle fibres. Once torn, inflexible scar tissue often fill the afflicted area, leaving it weak and always susceptible to further damage.

front stretch on bar

Though there are a diverse variety of stretches, the slow-hold form, or *static stretch*, is best. It is done by slowly stretching until a slight feeling of discomfort appears, and then holding that position for a period of fifteen to thirty seconds.

MTP flexibility training is performed with or without a partner. Some of the solo stretches include frontal bends on a bar, and performing a variety of splits with a power stretch apparatus. When working with a partner, elevating the leg as high as possible to the side is an effective method of improving flexibility, as is having him apply pressure as you bend forward to touch your chin to the floor.

power stretcher

high side stretch with partner

splits with partner

Endurance Training

The best endurance exercise is running. A normal running schedule for a serious mu tau pankration student is four to five days weekly, covering a minimum distance of three miles in twenty-four minutes or less. This includes different tempo and strides, usually mixing in full-speed bursts (sprints) for several yards with easier jogging. By running religiously, one conditions virtually all of the muscles in the body, as well as the heart, lungs, and circulation.

Another endurance exercise emphasized in the modern pankratiast's training agenda is rope-jumping, or rope-skipping. Rope-jumping not only develops stamina and strong leg muscles, but also brings about improvement in footwork, making you "light" on your feet.

rope-jumping

This exercise is controlled by the clock. In the early stages, rope-jumping is done for two, perhaps three, three-minute rounds with one-minute breaks. After greater skill and dexterity are achieved, the rest periods can be omitted and one can jump rope for ten to fifteen minutes nonstop.

There are basically two rhythms employed when rope-jumping. These rhythms relate primarily to the speed with which the rope is swung. Both rhythms can be performed either in series or in combination. The most frequently used rhythm is *single-time* or *pepper rhythm*. With this rhythm, the trainee makes a slight jump with each pass of the rope. *Double-time rhythm* requires a very fast swinging rope as well as a much higher jump. The rope makes two complete turns to pass twice beneath the feet with each jump.

Once the rope-jumping rhythms are perfected, the trainee must become well-versed in various patterns. From these, thousands of unique and creative routines are devised by each student.

Strength Training

The Greeks have long believed in using resistance to develop strength. Certain vase paintings show Athenian athletes exercising with very light weights for the purposes of improving their muscle tone and quickness. The tradition continues today.

All movement is a result of a muscle, or a group of muscles, contracting to produce movement. The intensity of a strike, kick, or grappling maneuver is determined by the joint effort of various muscle groups coordinating the technique. For example, a swift, powerful punch is not the product of just the arms. In many cases the power behind a punch is generated in the legs, by a stance or a shifting of weight. It is then transmitted through the torso by a slight waist twist, and is amplified by the arms, back, and shoulders. Essentially, the devastating punch or kick is the result of synchronized body movement rather than kinetic strength itself, but since a certain degree of strength will greatly enhance the end result, one should strive diligently to develop overall muscular strength.

The type of exercise that is appropriate for readying one's muscles for combat is quite different from that used to build muscular size. In any area of the fighting arts, the object is to harden and tone the muscles rather than building size or mass. The key to combat success lies in the application of efficient muscle power.

Strength training in MTP consists of using either free weights or the weight of the body to supply the resistive force necessary to increase bodily strength. Contrary to the old way of thinking in the martial arts, weight training is advantageous in developing power without loss of speed. One must be cautious, however, not to build large, bulky muscles which might sacrifice swiftness and flexibility. The key element in proper weight training for combat purposes is not in how much weight one can lift, but in doing the exercises correctly in full, smooth repetitions. For this reason, today's pankration trainees lift relatively lighter poundages in high reps (three sets of twelve to fifteen repetitions is a minimal workout for an exercise that isolates a specific muscle group).

The following exercises are representative of mu tau pankration strength training. The first set is designed to develop the neck and stomach muscles for the purpose of taking head and body shots in combat. The second group concentrates on improving punching power and upper body strength by developing those muscles directly used in both striking and grappling techniques.

NECK AND ABDOMINAL EXERCISES: In a full-contact combative art, powerful neck and abdominal muscles are necessary to withstand the shock impact of solid blows to the head and midsection. Boxers who suffer from frequent knockdowns or knockouts, referred to as having "glass jaws", can attribute their inability to take a punch on the chin to weak neck muscles. If the abdominal region of a fighter is not conditioned, he can easily get the wind knocked out of him from either a single well-placed blow or accumulation.

One means of building a strong neck is to perform isotonic *neck lifts* using a headstrap and weighted plate. An alternative method is to take a position on your hands and knees and attempt to lift your head upward against some immovable object, such as a heavy bag or a partner who uses both hands to supply resistance.

neck lifts with harness

160

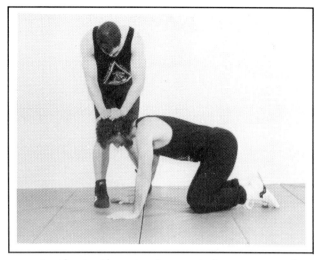

Neck bridging exercises are also part of the pankratiast's training regimen, as they are in all combat systems oriented to grappling. In the front bridge, the trainee places the top of his head on the mat and arches his back so that the feet and head are the sole supporting points. In the back bridge, the exercise is similar except that the trainee takes a supine position on the mat. The neck muscles are developed in both positions by rolling the head back and forth.

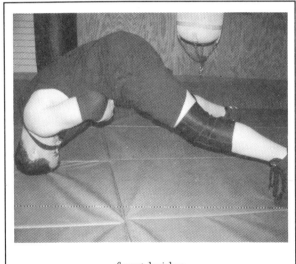

front bridge

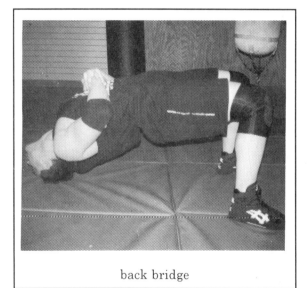

back bridge

There are several exercises to strengthen the abdominals, the most popular being *crunches*. Crunches are best for hardening the upper stomach muscles (rectus abdominis). In pankration training, this movement is always performed slowly with the upper body descending slower than ascending. More benefit is gained by doing them in a slow and deliberate manner as continuous tension is concentrated on the abs. The <u>quality</u> of the movement is more important in this exercise than the quantity. In other words, it is not the number of repetitions as many tend to think but the way in which the crunching movement is done.

To perform the crunch, a special device can be used which is designed to reduce the strain on the neck and concentrate all of the effort on the stomach. With the hands placed on both sides of the unit, the upper body is raised forward to a half-situp position. This movement is repeated several times until a burning sensation is felt in the abdominal area.

Other excellent abdominal building exercises are *situps* and *leg raises*. Situps, like crunches, work the upper abdominals whereas leg raises develop the lower muscles of the stomach, perhaps the most underworked area in the human body. Situps are more productive when using a slant board.

crunches

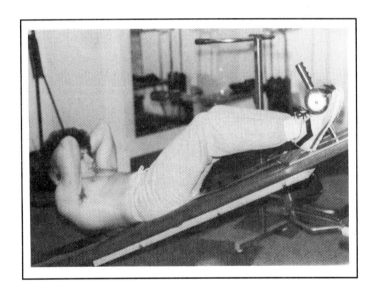

incline situps

In performing leg raises, the equipment required include a flat bench and ankle weights. The degree of difficulty in performing leg raises is regulated by how straight the legs are maintained. A more difficult variation of the leg raise are *slamdowns*, where the legs are elevated as high as possible and forced downward to the floor by a partner.

LEG RAISES

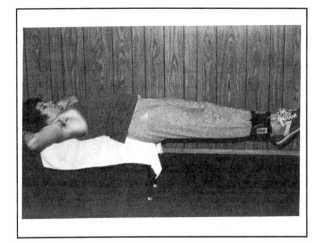 

SLAMDOWNS

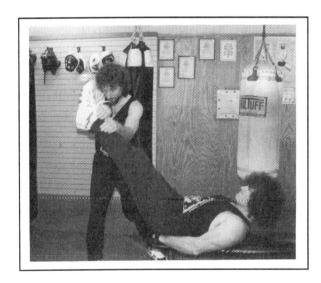 

To toughen the stomach region and, at the same time, simulate getting hit there, a *medicine ball* is used in mu tau pankration training. Weighing fifteen pounds or more, it is thrown forcefully by a partner against the front or side of the midsection. To vary this drill, the pankratiast can lie on his back and have a partner drop the ball on his stomach. If training alone, you can drop upon the ball with your stomach while doing pushups.

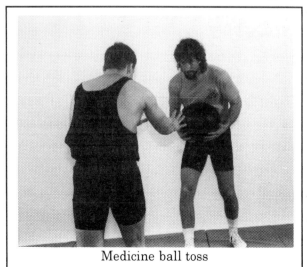

Medicine ball toss

Medicine ball drop

Medicine ball side slams

Medicine ball pushups.

WEIGHT TRAINING FOR UPPER BODY STRENGTH: Grappling
effectiveness, as well as punching power, is dependent on leverage and the combined effort of various muscles, namely the forearms, the triceps, the pectorals (chest), and the deltoids (shoulders). Prior to the delivery of a blow or application of a grip or takedown, each set of muscles is in a relaxed state, and instantly contracted at the exact moment of contact. The stronger muscle will produce a faster, more responsive contraction which, in turn, results in a more forceful action.

An excellent weight training exercise for the forearm muscles is the *reverse curl*. The reverse curl works on the outside and top of the forearm, the lower portion of the arm that provides the "driving" force for many of the punching techniques employed in this fighting art. A special bar, called an E-Z Curl bar, is an absolute must for this exercise to really lock all of the action into the forearms. The angles of the bar isolate the forearm muscles, forcing them to work synergistically so that only forearm strength and muscle perform the exercise.

Another forearm developer is the *wrist roll*. The equipment used in this tough exercise consists of a ten-pound weight attached to a cylindrical handle by a rope or cord. The length of the cord is such that the weight be at the level of the thighs when completely unwound. Standing erect, the arms are raised straight out and the elbows locked, palms down. The elbows are not bent at any time. Without the arms moving, the cord is then wound up steadily on the handle by using only a wrist action. Both hands must equally raise the weight. Once the weight touches the hands, the cord is slowly unwound to lower the weight.

To develop the inside of the forearms, *leverage bar rotations* are considered the best method. Using the dumbbell weighted on one end and using an overhand grip, the trainee twists his wrist back and forth.

The triceps, muscles located on the outer side of the upper arm, are also essential in punching and many grappling techniques. This muscle group is the one used in pushing movements and, since the muscle involved in punching is the same as in pushing, exercises to develop this area are commonplace in pankration training. The best triceps exercise is *dips*. Using parallel bars, the trainee drops his body slowly and then presses upward. The legs are bent at all times and the body is held erect.

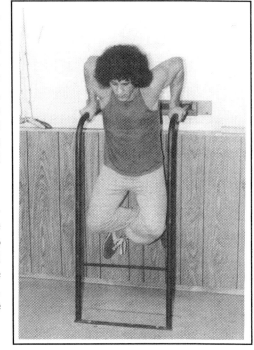

As this is essentially a triceps developer, one must be careful to maintain the proper form. If the trainee leans forward too much, for example, it becomes a strict pectoral (chest) workout. One must always give it the full repetition, going all the way up and down. The more fully the movement is made, the more fully the muscle is developed.

OTHER WEIGHT TRAINING EXERCISES

Elevated pushups (triceps)

Behind-the-neck press
(deltoids)

Bench press
(chest/triceps)

Flyes (chest)

BASIC DRILLS

Breakfall and Rolling Exercises

Practice in breaking one's fall and rolling is essential to grapplers. It teaches one to soften the shock of falling when the body's balance is lost. It is also a means of using the force movement of the opponent, following its direction while avoiding the resistance of the ground. The most common of these exercises are:

Simple Back Fall: Crouch at the knees, and let yourself roll gently back. Strike the mat forcefully with your arms just before your back hits the mat. Your head should NOT hit the mat.

Simple Side Fall: Raise one leg, pivoting to the side, and roll back on your buttocks. Slap the mat hard with your nearest arm just prior to your back hitting the mat.

  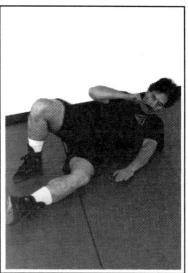

Simple Forward Fall: Drop gently to your knees, then fall forward. Slap the mat with your hands and forearms. Keep your hands directly in front of your face, and the elbows turned slightly outward. Only the toes, knees, and forearms should touch the mat.

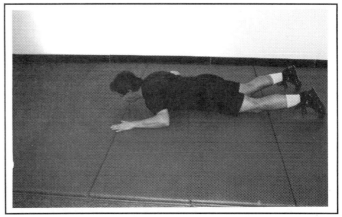

Basic Forward Roll: With feet shoulder-width apart, place your left hand straight in front of you, with the right slightly behind it. Distribute your weight onto your left foot and left hand. Raise your right foot, and roll down your left arm, onto the shoulder, back, and right side, slapping the mat with the right arm and leg at the completion of the fall.

Spinning Drill

The spinning drill develops agility and quick, nimble movement for the pankratiast once he has secured top control on the ground. It is done by having a partner maintain a stationary position with his hands and knees planted on the mat and his head held low. The top man plants his chest and full weight directly on his partner's back, with legs well spread and toes touching the mat. The arms are extended outward. Once the command "spin' is given, the top man will rotate his body using his chest to pivot on the bottom man's back. He never crosses his legs while spinning, nor do his hands make contact with his partner's body. At random, the bottom participant will lift either arm to block the top man's direction, forcing him to rotate the other way.

Skiamachia

Skiamachia (Greek: to fight with shadows) is an ancient form of freestyle shadow-boxing which was popular among both Greek boxers and pankratiasts. It is used primarily to practice upright fighting skills such as punching combinations, footwork, kicking, and defenses. The modern practitioner often utilizes a mirror, thereby reflecting his own image as a target or imaginary opponent. The mirror is particularly helpful in examining one's movements for flaws such as telegraphed blows.

Skiamachia improves form, balance, speed, and coordination as opposed to a powerful punch. Since the MTP trainee is striking the air and not a solid object, he must be careful not to hyperextend his limbs when executing his techniques or injuries will result. In addition, the practitioner must be creative and spontaneous. Skiamachia is not in any way a prearranged form where memorization and strict mechanical precision are critical to execution. The emphasis is more like that in Greek dance, with freedom of expression and fluid, unplanned movement the key factors. Such practice better enables one to react instinctively to the uncertainties he will face in an actual combat situation.

This training is timed in three-minute rounds with one-minute breaks. If performed properly, shadow-fighting can also benefit one's cardiovascular system.

Offense-Defense Drills

In these drills, a student will attack with various offensive techniques while his partner defends without retaliation. Both strikes and takedown attempts are employed in one's attack. The defender can execute any defensive action, be it a parry against a punch, a block against a kick, or a sprawl against a leg tackle.

SPARRING

Sparring, or free-fighting, with full contact and protective gear heads the list on the mu tau pankration training plan. There is really no better practice in developing one's proficiency in combat. Sparring serves as the "testing ground" for one's techniques and for one's ability to withstand punishment. Only this type of activity offers the practitioner a realistic opportunity (second only to actual combat) to express and explore himself, and to discover what works and what does not. It is the best means of keeping one's skills and reflexes fine-tuned.

There are no set rules that govern an MTP open sparring session. For the most part, pankratiasts go at it with few restrictions. The participants wear protective gear, and are encouraged to hit and kick from shin to head, and to freely apply grappling and ground-fighting techniques from in close. The duration of a free sparring match is arranged in advance by both fighters or by their trainer, and usually consist of ten minutes of non-stop action. A boundary, such as a boxing ring, may be used to contain the fighters. Not treated as a contest, there are no points awarded, no referees, and no declaration of a winner. A match can be terminated at any time by a knockout rendered from a kick, strike, elbow, or knee blow; or by any grappling submission hold. The sparmates realize well ahead of time that this training is a type of experimental analysis which attempts, as closely as possible, to duplicate the potential conditions of combat in the street.

To minimize the risk of serious injury, the pankratiasts wear headgear, mouthpieces, and groin cups, as well as special fight gloves with fingers to facilitate grappling techniques. Knee padding is also worn to protect the knees from abrasions, often incurred during ground fighting.

One will not deny the exhaustive and grueling effect this training has on the human body. However, this is representative of mu tau's insistence on properly preparing a strong, well-conditioned athlete for combat. And those entering this phase with some irrational self-image of invincibility quickly discover the error of such thinking. Everyone who spars under MTP conditions will be hit, kicked, and taken down. The goal is to minimize the effect of each of these actions while maximizing those of your own. A student quickly discovers to adapt to a fight's unpredictability, while testing his knowledge, courage, and physical attributes. For those who undertake the study of the art, this is the foremost learning experience.

Sparring is an absolute necessity for those who compete in limited rules fighting events. What follows are the basic rules observed by the participants in contemporary "all-powers" combat contests sanctioned by the **UPA** (United Pankration Alliance).

Basic UPA Contest Rules

- Fighters are classified as either AMATEUR or PROFESSIONAL according to competitive experience in sanctioned pankration-rules bouts.

  AMATEUR: Novice (0 - 4 bouts), Intermediate (5 - 8 bouts with a minimum of 1 win at Novice class), Advanced (9 - 14 bouts with a minimum of 2 wins at Intermediate class).

  PROFESSIONAL: 15+ bouts with a minimum of 2 wins at Advanced class.

- Strikes permitted include any punch, kick, knee strike, or combination thereof, to the face or body of an upright fighter; and blows with the fist, foot, or knee to the body of a contestant on the ground.

- Leg kicks and stomping on the feet are permitted.

- All grappling techniques in the form of takedowns, throws, joint locks, or chokeholds are permitted.

- No eye-gouging, biting, groin shots, blows to the face of an opponent on the ground, "fish-hooking" (putting fingers in opponent's mouth), tearing or pulling the ear, stomping on the face, head, or body, elbowing, or headbutts.

- The duration of amateur matches are 5 continuous minutes with championship bouts 10 continuous minutes. Professional matches are 15 continuous minutes with championship bouts 20 continuous minutes.

- Fighters shall wear lightweight leather open-finger gloves, mouthpiece, groin cup, knee pads, full-face headgear, elbow pads (optional), and wrestling shoes.

- A winner is declared by one of the following:

  KNOCKOUT (KO). A knockdown is counted if a competitor goes down from the impact of a blow (not a push, slip, or throw). The referee will signal the fighter who struck the blow to a neutral corner and initiate a 10-count. If the downed fighter cannot return to his feet before the end of the 10-count, the bout is ruled a KO. A KO is also ruled when an opposing fighter is choked unconscious.

  SUBMISSION. Fighter signals defeat or indicates no desire to continue. This is done by "tapping out" (slapping with open palm multiple times on the mat or the opponent), or verbally.

  TECHNICAL KNOCKOUT (TKO). Coach/cornerman throws in the towel, fighter verbally quits, or ring judge calls the match due to excessive bleeding or if a fighter is unable to adequately defend himself).

  A **DRAW** (no-decision) shall be called if any of these three decisions above is not attained.

- The fighting area shall be no less than a 16-foot square ring or matted area.

- The match is not halted nor are the fighters separated in the event of a clinch or fall to the mat.

- The ring judge may stop a fight in case of unsportsmanlike conduct or an infraction of any rule.

- There are six (6) weight divisions recognized in UPA-sanctioned bouts:

  Lightweight (under 140 pounds)   **Welterweight** (141 - 160 pounds)
  Middleweight (161 - 180 pounds)   **Light Heavyweight** (181 - 195 pounds)
  Heavyweight (196 - 220 pounds)   **Super Heavyweight** (221+ pounds)

GLOSSARY

α. MU TAU PANKRATION TERMINOLOGY

The following are some of the most frequently used Greek and English terms and abbreviations spoken in an MTP training facility.

A

ACADEMY: School, training gym, institute.

ADAPTABILITY: The ability to react spontaneously to meet the everchanging, unpredictable conditions of combat.

ADVANTAGE, Position of: In grappling, having the top position on the opposing fighter.

AFENDI: Greek terminology for "Teacher" or "Instructor."

AGG-KOHN: Greek: elbow.

AGGRESSOR: A classification of fighter who continually leads and presses the offensive action.

AIDOS: Honorable sportsmanship without arrogance.

AKONITI: Greek term for a "walk-over" victory (no-contest).

AMPHOTIDES: Greek term for headgear. Were helmets worn in sparring practice by ancient pankratiasts to protect the head from injury.

ANGLING: A tactical positioning of the body in relation to that of one's opponent. This positioning is a crucial factor in delivering a successful attack. The angle of entry, as it is often called, can be of three variations: straight-on, flank (inside/outside), or rear.

ANO PANKRATION: Upright fighting similar to kickboxing which specializes in striking techniques with fists, feet, elbows, and knees.

ARETE: Greek for manly or martial value.

A.T.: Aggression Transfer. The capability of a trained modern pankratiast to transmit psychological hatred for his opponent into his physical techniques. Requires proper anger-provoking mental stimulation while actual striking and kicking drills are in progress.

AUDIO PERCEPTION: The ability to anticipate an unseen, surprise action through a highly-developed sense of hearing. Often consists of blind-folded training drills.

B

BALANCE: The physical attribute that enables an athlete to maintain good alignment both in a static position as well as during motion.

BLITZING: Any swift, abrupt inward rush which is usually accompanied by a barrage of heavy punches or a takedown.

BODY BLASTING: A heavy, concentrated punching assault on the opponent's midsection.

BOB & WEAVE: An up and down, side to side swaying motion of the shoulders and head employed at close range combat. Is both defensive and aggressive in nature. It makes the fighter extremely difficult to hit squarely and adds power to his short punches (hooks and uppercuts).

BROKEN RHYTHM: A sudden, unexpected variation in one's offense either in the form of a change of direction or altering the set pace (rhythm) with which the techniques are made. Results in a disruption in the opponent's sense of timing.

BLOCKING: Taking a blow on the gloves, arms, or shoulders.

BODY BANGING: A training drill for hardening the torso through the use of padded gloves or a medicine ball.

BOXE FRANCAISE SAVATE: A form of French boxing characterized by extensive use of the feet to deliver blows.

BREAKDOWN: A grappling move in which the fighter flattens an opponent to the ground on his stomach or side, usually when he is in the bottom position.

BRIDGING THE GAP: An expression commonly employed for closing the spacial relationship (distance) between fighters in order to land a blow or execute a takedown. Bridging the gap and attacking are generally simultaneous actions.

BUTTING: Using the head to strike the opponent.

C

CADENCE: Speed regulated to coincide with that of the opponent. It is a specific rhythm at which a succession of movements is executed.

CAESTUS: An addition by the Romans to their combat sports events. It essentially armed the fighters with a lethal spiked and weighted glove which replaced the athletic skill inspired by the Greeks with an increase in brutality and death.

CATCH: A fundamental block for a jab lead.

CENTERLINE: The imaginary wide line running down the middle of the body. The centerline forms the theoretical nucleus of attack and defense and must be protected at all times.

CENTRAL VISION: A type of visual focusing in which the eyes and attention are fixed on one point.

CHAMBERING: Bringing the leg to the cocked position just prior to kicking to attain maximum speed and power in the kick's delivery.

CHANCERY: A popular ancient pankration technique involving the pulling of the hair to gain leverage for one's blows, or gaining release from a grappling hold.

CLASSICAL WAY: A traditional martial arts system that remains fixed in time and does not flow with the constant change of our progressive culture.

CLINCH: At close range, grabbing the opponent by the legs, waist, or around the neck. Usually is a starting point for knee strikes or grappling action.

COMBINATION: Is a fluid sequence of two or more blows, or strategic attacks.

COMBOS: Slang often used for combinations.

COMPLEMENTING FORCE: Flowing in the direction that the force is being generated rather than against it. Often applied in grappling situations and on defense.

COMPLEX ATTACK: Not a simple maneuver but one requiring more energy and movements such as any spinning-type attack.

CONTROL: The authority or power to regulate or dominate a situation, such as a grappling hold or the course of a fight itself.

COUNTER: Is a blow or grappling technique given in response to an opponent's lead. Another of the recognized mu tau pankration methods of strategically deploying the tools.

COVER: Raising the arms to protect against hooking punches to the head.

CRITICAL DISTANCE: The range at which an attack **must** be made.

CRITICAL TARGET: A vulnerable spot of the human anatomy which, when correctly struck, causes the greatest damage to one's opponent. The eyes and groin are examples of critical targets.

CROSS-STEP: A type of offensive footwork used to deliver certain mu tau pankration kicking tools.

CROUCHER: A fighter who does battle with his stance lowered and his upper body bent forward.

CURVED LINE: The path taken for circular-type blows such as hooking punches and kicks.

D

DARTING: Rapid, crisp in and out moves usually for scoring quick jabs.

DECEPTION: A decoy or false movement used to elicit a response from the opponent. Applied in the Indirect Attack.

DEFLECTION: A sharp, well-timed slap of the palm to the inside, outside, or onto an oncoming blow or kick, to divert the assault from its original path.

DISCIPLE: A follower or student of the art.

DISTANCING: The amount of space between fighters.

DISTRACTION: See Deception.

DODGING: An evasive form of footwork involving lateral movement, to the inside or outside of an oncoming blow.

DOUBLE-LEG TAKEDOWN: A takedown maneuver whereby both of the opponent's legs are gripped.

DUCKING: A defensive evasion for escaping hooks and swings to the head by dropping the body forward.

E

EFFICIENCY: A technique that is functional without wasting energy or movement.

ELEVATOR: An escape move employed against a top-mounted opponent which features arching the back and legs when trapped on the bottom.

ELUSIVE: A constantly-moving target which is difficult to hit or take down to the ground.

ENDURANCE: The ability of the body to perform work over long periods of time.

ENVIRONMENTAL TRAINING: Training that deals with acclimating the student with his surroundings when engaged in combat.

ESCAPE: Gaining a neutral position after being controlled in a grappling position or hold.

EXPLOSIVENESS: The action of abruptly bursting forth or releasing energy from a prior state of relative calm.

EXTRAPOLATE: To tactically predict an opponent's response to a certain move on the basis of previous responses to the same movement.

EVASION: To avoid an oncoming blow or kick by a precisely timed head, body, or foot movement, thereby allowing the hands to be free to retaliate.

F

FAKES: Body gestures such as movements of the eyes, head, and shoulders used to disguise an intended attack.

FEINT: A pretense of attack to one area and delivering the actual blow to another by means of false limb movements (i.e. hand & foot feints).

FLANK: Angling one's body to the inside or outside position of the opponent's front foot.

FLUIDITY: The capability of performing techniques smoothly and with the utmost ease.

FOCUS: Zeroing in on a small target area with a maximum of force.

FOLLOW-THROUGH: Driving the fist or foot internally, several inches beyond the target area. Mu tau pankration blows vary in depth or follow-through.

FOUL TACTICS: Those combat techniques which have no precise, teachable form but are the result of pure survival instinct. Includes biting, ear and hair pulling, eye gouging, etc.

FREESTYLE WRESTLING: An open style of amateur wrestling where the contestants are allowed the full use of their bodies to score points or pin their opponent.

G

GASTRIZEIN: Greek for "stomach kick."

GRAPPLING: Another term for wrestling. Consists of takedowns, joint locks, submission chokeholds, and other maneuvers.

GRECO-ROMAN WRESTLING: A major style of wrestling used in international competition as well as the Olympic Games in which the use of the feet or legs is limited.

GUARD: (1)The placement of one's arms in the readiness position, or (2) A defensive position on the ground in which the fighter's legs are scissored about the opponent's waist, restricting his offensive ability from the top mount.

GYMNASTES: In ancient Greece, an athletic trainer.

GYO: Greek for "knee strike."

GRON-THOS: Greek for striking with the open hand or closed fist.

H

HALF-COMMITTED THRUST: A partially-executed blow employed to evoke a response from one's opponent. Akin to feinting.

HEAD HUNTER: A striker who delivers his blows solely to the head.

HEAD SHOT: A blow aimed at the head.

HEART: Refers to a fighter's inner drive to win at all costs.

HEAVE: An ancient grappling technique sometimes used to counter a leg takedown. It involves gripping the opponent about the waist, lifting him, and dropping him on his head, resulting in a broken neck.

HEAVY ARTILLERY: Mu tau pankration's arsenal of full-powered penetrating blows and kicks.

HIGH LINE: The area of the human anatomy above shoulder level.

HIMANTES: Hand wraps of soft oxide worn by ancient Greek boxers

HOPLOMACHOS: Greek "weapons specialists."

HYPTIASMOS: Greek for "back-fall."

I

INFIGHTING: Combat action at close quarters. Elbowing, kneeing, and grappling techniques are favored offensive weapons at this range.

INITIATION SPEED: The rapidity with which a technique or movement is triggered from readiness.

INSIDE HAND RANGE: The distance from which compact, bent-arm hand blows are delivered.

INTERCEPTION: A blow or kick delivered as the opponent is in the process of launching a blow of his own.

ISOLATED SPARRING: A developmental type of sparring drill which restricts the participants to a certain technique or set of techniques.

J

JAMMING: A means of obstructing a kicking attempt by sensing the impending attack and then moving in close before the kick has had any real chance of gaining any impetus. Especially effective against the fighter who emphasizes kicks in his offense.

JOINT LOCK: A grappling technique featuring any type of painful grip or hold upon the opponent's joints (i.e. wrist, elbow, knee, ankle, etc.).

K

KATO PALE: Greek term for "ground wrestling."

KATO PANKRATION: A rougher and more comprehensive form of the art emphasizing everything-goes ground combat. Was the form preferred in the ancient Olympic games.

KEE-REE-OS: Greek for "Grandmaster" or "Founder" of the system.

KLIMAKISMOS: Greek for "ladder trick." Is a grappling maneuver wherein a fighter jumps on his opponent's back and applies a choke while scissoring his abdomen at the same time.

KLIMAX: An agreement between fighters to trade blows without blocking them until one fighter dropped and a clear-cut winner was declared.

K.O.: Short for <u>K</u>nock-<u>O</u>ut. Refers to rendering an opponent unconscious by a blow, kick, or grappling assault.

KORYKEOIN: A special room in the palaestra equipped with training apparatus for boxers and pankratiasts.

KORYKOS: Greek terminology for "suspended heavy bags."

L

LAK-TEE-ZO: Greek for "kicking/striking with the foot."

LATENT DISTRACTION: A distractive body or limb movement comprised of feints and fakes.

LATERAL MOVEMENT: Refer to sidestepping or dodging.

LEAD: The initial attack. Normally a characteristic of the more aggressive fighter.

LEFT STANCER: See Orthodox Position.

LEVERAGE: Positioning the body in such a manner that the greatest amount of physical force can be generated into the blow or grappling maneuver.

LIMB SHOTS: Blows delivered to the arms or legs.

LINEAR MOVEMENT: Straight forward or backward movement (i.e. advancing/retreating).

LOW LINE: The area of the human anatomy from the waist down.

LONG RANGE: The distance beyond arm's reach of an adversary in which kicks are the most effective offensive weapons.

LURING: See Drawing.

M

MANIFEST DISTRACTION: Any unexpected noise resulting in a momentary reduction in body coordination.

MID-LINE: The area of the anatomy from waist level to the shoulders.

MOBILITY: Continual, unpredictable movement.

MOMENTUM: The product of the mass (weight) and velocity of a moving body. Also referred to as "impetus."

MOUNT: The top control position assumed in ground fighting.

MTP: An abbreviation for "Mu Tau Pankration."

MUAY-THAI: A form of boxing practiced in Thailand, allowing the use of fists, feet, elbows, and knees in knockout bouts.

MU TAU: A Grecian acronym coined in 1970 by Jim Arvanitis for **Martial Truth**. Is an eclectic collection of techniques and training methodology combined with the nucleus concepts of the classic Greek pankration.

N

NHB: An abbreviation for "No-Holds-Barred" fighting.
NON-CLASSICAL: Not saturated with traditional theory and ritual. Progressive and everchanging.

O

O-D DRILLS: Drills whereby one trainee only attacks, and the other concentrates solely on defense.
ONE-FOUR: A numbering scheme for a jab lead and uppercut combination.
ONE-FOUR-THREE: A 3-punch series of lead jab, uppercut, and hook.
ONE-THREE: Another numbered punching combination for a hook punch off of a jab lead.
ONE-TWO: A numbering scheme for a jab and reverse thrust punching combination.
ONE-TWO-THREE: A numbered 3-punch combination for a jab, rear thrust, and hook punch.
ORTHIA PALE: Greek for "upright wrestling." Includes clinching, takedowns, and throwing techniques.
ORTHODOX POSITION: A position of combat readiness in which the left hand and left foot are placed forward.
OUTFIGHTING: See Long Range.
OUTSIDE HAND RANGE: The distance from which straight-line punches, such as the lead jab and reverse thrust, are employed.

P

PACING: A means of actively (physically and mentally) regulating the output of energy during the course of combat or running long distances.
PALAESTRA: Greek for "training hall."
PAIDOTRIBES: In ancient Greece, a trainer of unarmed combat.
PALE: Greek term for "wrestling."
PAMMACHON: Greek for "total fight"; an old term for integrated combat used prior to the sport of pankration.
PANKRATION: Literally translated from the Greek as "all powers." Was an ancient Greek combative practice which was introduced into the Olympic games of 648 B.C. Is the primary foundation upon which the mu tau style evolved.
PARRY: See Deflection.

PARTIALITY: An inclination to favoring "this" over "that" such as straight lines over curves, kicking over striking, etc. Infers the inability to comprehend "total fighting freedom."

PASSIVE BLOCKING: A classical defense in which hard, rigid blocks are performed with one arm while the other arm is placed passively at the hip.

PENETRATION: See Follow-Through.

PERIPHERAL VISION: Visual focusing in combat whereby the eyes are fixed on one point as attention expands to a greater area.

PILEDRIVER: Refer to "Heave."

PIVOT: A turning of the body to attain maximum power in one's blows. Various pivoting maneuvers are employed for specific MTP techniques, such as hook punching and back-leg round kicks.

PUG-LAK: Greek term for "kickboxing"; the use of hands and feet to fight.

PNEUMA: Greek for "inner strength." Comparable in meaning to the Japanese *ki*, Chinese *chi*, Indian *prana*, etc.

POLEMIKOS: Greek for "one who fights"; a martial artist.

POSITIONING: Refers to the placement of the head and limbs in one's on-guard fighting pose.

PO-THEE: Greek for "foot."

PREPARATION: Readying oneself both mentally and physically for unrestrained combat conditions.

PRIMARY TOOLS: The most fundamental techniques of the art.

PROBING: Investigating and analyzing the opponent's reactions through exploratory actions.

PROGRESSIVE: Non-classical; modern; constantly evolving with fresh ideas relative to combat realism.

PROTECTIVE SHELL: A defensive cover assumed during infighting.

PUGME: Greek term for "boxing."

PULSATING RHYTHM: A perpetual movement that recurs alternately or in regulated sequence. Developed chiefly through training to music.

PYRRHIC: In ancient Greece, dancelike exercises practiced with weaponry that resembled actual fighting movements.

R

RAPID-FIRE DELIVERY: Swift execution of hits and kicks based on an absolute minimum of movement.

REACTION SPEED: The rapidity with which physical responses are made to an opponent's moves.

READINESS: A state of super alertness from one's guard position.

RECOVERY: The action of coming back strong after an initial attack has landed.

REFLEX ACTION: Instantaneous responsiveness, without thinking, to an opponent's physical actions.

RELEASE: Escaping from a grappling hold or submission technique.

RETREAT: To back away from an attack.

REVERSAL: In grappling, the altering of a control situation.

RIDING: Refers to controlling an opponent from the top position.

RIGHT STANCER: See Southpaw Position.

ROADWORK: A running technique used to develop stamina.

ROLLOUT: In grappling, an escape move by which you roll rapidly with force in the same direction that your opponent's weight is concentrated.

ROOTS: The early beginnings or foundation upon which a progressive art is based. For example, early pankration concepts are the roots of MTP.

ROTATING MOVEMENT: Circling one's adversary in a tactical process of probing for openings and changing angles.

ROUND: A fighting period, lasting two or three minutes in duration.

RUNNER: The classification of that fighter who continually hits and retreats.

S

SALUTE: Greek for salutation. In modern pankration is comprised of placing the palm side of the closed right fist over the upper left chest area.

SAVATE: See Boxe Francaise Savate.

SENIOR TRAINER: A teaching rank indicative of superior experience, knowledge, and skill. Authorized to supervise all mu tau pankration training sessions.

SET-UPS: A series of preliminary actions, including feints, that lead into major attacks.

SET PATTERNS: Prearranged training drills, such as **kata** and **one-step/two-step sparring**. Characteristic of the classical Asian martial arts.

SHARPENING THE TOOLS: Improving the speed, power, and accuracy of one's technique's through regular training. Involves the utilization of various punching and kicking equipment.

SHIFTY: A movement characteristic of the fighter skilled in lateral movement.

SHUFFLE: Moving on the balls of the feet. Not flat-footed.

SIG-MA: MTP title for "Senior Trainer."

SIMPLICITY: The essence of MTP's approach to combat, especially in terms of technical elements. Instead of loading up its arsenal with complicated moves, MTP places emphasis on simple, practical attacks and defenses that can be relied upon to do the job effectively.

SINGLE LEG TAKEDOWN: A takedown attempt in which the assault is directed toward only one of the opponent's legs.

SKIAMACHIA: Greek terminology for "shadow-fighting." A favored form of training by ancient Greek boxers and pankratiasts. Is the practice of fighting moves without an opponent.

SLIDE: An offensive type of footwork where the rear foot "hops" inward thereby bridging the gap suddenly and swiftly.

SLIPPING: Avoiding a blow by moving the head to the left or right without moving the body out of range.

SOUTHPAW: The ready position in which the right hand and right foot are placed forth.

SPACING: See Distancing.

SPHAIRAI: Greek for "padded gloves."

SPRAWL: A rapid evasive maneuver to avoid being grasped by the legs; initiated when the opposing fighter dives in low to attempt a takedown.

SPRINGINESS: A quality of combat movement made possible by slightly bending the knees and raising the heels.

STAMINA: See Endurance.

STAA-MAH-TA: Greek for "halt/stop."

STANCE: The positioning of the lower body (feet and legs) in one's ready pose.

STEP-THROUGH: Offensive footwork used in the delivery of specific mu tau pankration kicks.

STRATEGY: A mental planning of actions or maneuvers used to gain an edge over an opponent. Is a quality of an intelligent fighter.

STRIKING RANGE: The fighting distance from which blows and kicks can reach an opponent's critical targets.

SUBMISSION HOLD: A lock or hold upon an opponent's neck or joints that forces him to surrender or else suffer strangulation or a broken limb. Such a technique is cause for terminating an all-out sparring match.

SURVIVAL INSTINCT: An internal drive that is not easily learned and that results in an attitude to win at all costs. Compare to "Heart."

SWAYING MOVEMENT: See Bobbing and Weaving.

SUSTAINED ATTACK: To keep up or maintain a steady offensive onslaught, usually with the same technique.

T

TACTICS: Well-planned actions and steps taken to ultimately conquer the opposition. It is the strategic ability of a fighter to meet and successfully solve problems as they arise in combat. They are NOT preconceived notions but are part of on-going process which continues until the battle ends. They are primarily concerned with avoiding the opponent's strengths and exploiting his weaknesses.

TACKLE: See Takedown.

TAKEDOWN: A grappling technique whereby the opponent is knocked off his feet and placed him in a helpless situation against a follow-up offensive.

TELEGRAPH: A signal of one's intended actions, such as a dropping of the shoulder or the windup of the arm prior to delivering a punch.

TEMPO: Refers to the rate of speed at which a fighter makes any physical or combat movement. Variation in tempo, such as a sudden speeding up of an attack, is often an effective tactic in catching the opponent off-guard. Tempo is also applicable in exercises such as running and rope-jumping where change of output is essential.

THRATT-TO-MAY: Greek for "grappling."

TIE-UPS: See Clinch.

TIMING: Is the sudden reaction/response to a stimulus. It includes the capability to seize the exact moment for executing an action.

TOE-TO-TOE: A commonly used expression for infighting.

TOOLS: A term used to encompass the diverse technical elements of the art. Broken down into **hand tools**, **foot tools**, **infighting tools**, and **defensive tools**.

TORQUE: The capacity of a force for producing twisting or rotation, such as turning the hips into a power punch for greater striking impact. Compare with Leverage.

TOTALITY: Not partial in nature, as in a "style", but including all ways and means to carry out an objective.

TRANSITION: Closing the distance from one specified range to another. For instance, making the transition from punching range to grappling range.

TRAP: Holding down and checking the use of an opponent's arm so it cannot be employed for purposes of offense and defense.

TRIP: A takedown finish in which the opponent's leg or foot is blocked or kicked out from under him.

U

UNPREDICTABILITY: Making all physical actions a surprise to one's opponent. Never doing something in an expected manner.

V

VELOCITY: The speed with which an object, such as the hand, foot, or body, moves in a specified direction.

VISUAL PERCEPTION: The ability to use trained eyesight to gauge distance, uncover open targets upon which to score, and detect aggressive actions and moves before they can impart damage.

VULNERABLE POINT: Refers to any area of the body prone to disabling results when struck precisely. Compare to Critical Target.

Z

ZONE: A section of the body used as a target for one's blows and kicks. Refer to High, Medium, and Low Lines.

GREEK NUMBERING SYSTEM (1 - 10)

1/ehnah	6/ehksee
2/theeoh	7/ehfthah
3/treeah	8/ohkhthoh
4/tehsehrah	9/ehnyah
5/pehndeh	10/thehkah

β. MU TAU PANKRATION RANKINGS

Unlike various Asian martial arts styles, there are no colored belts awarded in Hellenic self-defense. In the ancient combat sports, a practitioner was considered either a student, a competing fighter, or a teacher *(paidotribes)*. In mu tau pankration, however, a unique ranking system based on experience, athletic skill, and dedication is recognized. It consists of the following ten grade levels (abbreviated as GLs) and are signified by colored emblems. The MTP emblem depicts two classic pankratiasts locked in ground combat bordered by the Greek *kee.*

The emblem of MTP

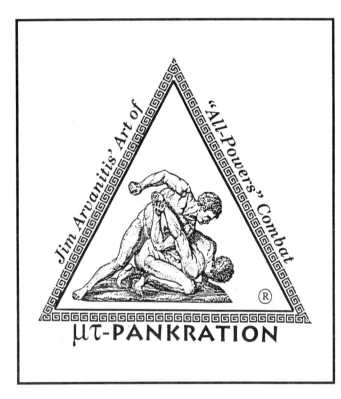

Ranking	Emblem Color
GL1/NoviceI	white
GL2/NoviceII	yellow
GL3/IntermediateI	green
GL4/IntermediateII	blue
GL5/AdvancedI	royal
GL6/AdvancedII	purple
GL7/Associate Instructor	brown
GL8/ Instructor	silver
GL9/Senior Instructor	red
GL10/Master	gold

All rankings are authorized by a certificate issued by the *Spartan Academy of Martial Arts* with the signatures of the student's immediate instructor. The colored rank emblem is part of the practitioner's formal uniform and is worn on the training jacket. It usually requires 7 years of training to attain the rank of instructor (GL8), and at least 12 years to reach senior instructor level. These timelines will vary based on individual effort and skill. Those seeking promotion to GL8 must not only possess fighting and teaching proficiency but must be highly-knowledgeable in pankration history and MTP terminology.

The following are officially-recognized grade levels of those practitioners currently authorized to teach the art of mu tau pankration in the U.S.A. These individuals are located primarily on the east coast.

Rank/Grade Level	Name
SENIOR INSTRUCTOR (GL9)	Nick Hines
INSTRUCTOR (GL8)	Mark Nash Douglas M. Terry Joseph Packard Steve Vaillas
ASSOCIATE INSTRUCTOR (GL7)	James Hines Eric Hill James Cross Rocco Caprarello David DeJohn Bruce Huckins Alexander Macreanis

χ. MTP ATTRIBUTES

Attributes refer to the dynamics that shape technique, and the inner qualities that separate the great martial artist from the average one. It can include anything from a blow that is felt but not seen, to one's resistance to accepting defeat at the hands of his adversary. Past pankration champions, such as Arrichion and Dioxippus, possessed these attributes, referred to as *pneuma* by the ancient Greeks. Attributes are certainly more than just physical skills, but encompass both the physical and mental characteristics that elevate an individual to the realm of superiority in his chosen craft.

PHYSICAL ATTRIBUTES

1. Strength

- Refers to the effort one can exert with a single maximal muscle contraction.
- Strength is definitely an asset to the MTP fighter, especially during close range combat. Success in grappling is frequently due to one's effective use of his strength.
- Strength is developed by specialized weight training and heavy bag workouts.

2. *Speed*

- Is comprised of the following elements -- quickness of the eye to spot openings; quickness of mind to select the right move at the proper time; quickness of reflexive action to react explosively and without hesitation; quickness of hand and foot in executing the chosen technique instantly and effectively.

- Economy of motion and relaxed muscles enhance speed. Wasted movements, overall tension, and unnecessary muscular contractions reduce speed and dissipate energy.

- Speed in hitting refers to how fast a blow covers distance to get to its target. It includes sudden initiation (no telegraphing) and a maximum acceleration up to the moment of impact. Regardless of distance, the final phase of the striking movement should be the fastest.

- Speed is instantaneous. Any deliberation in one's movements will definitely serve as detrimental to speed potential.

- Speed development drills include the use of the platform bag, T&B bag, focus gloves, and various sparring activities.

3. *Power*

- Is a combination of both strength and speed. It implies the ability to develop fast, explosive movements against resistance.

- Power is also dependent on leverage, positioning the body in such a way that the body drives the blow, kick, or grappling maneuver and is not the product of mere arm or leg strength alone.

- Power is enforced by tensing the working muscles at the moment of impact and not a second before.

- It is essential that the various muscle groups and tendons involved in the movement are kept loose and relaxed prior to contact. If the muscles already tense, they cannot be further tensed when impact is made. Tensing either too early or too late will diminish hitting force.

- A powerful blow is a penetrating one. It goes "through" the target, not just to it! The idea is to focus on "driving" the fist or foot several inches behind the target, utilizing mind and body together.

- Power development drills make use of the heavy bag, kick pads, etc.

4. *Coordination*

- Refers to the synchronized interaction between the body's nervous and muscular systems. This function is important for producing skillful movement.

- The well-coordinated fighter performs his techniques smoothly and gracefully. He makes purposeful actions with a minimum of effort and a maximum of speed and power.

- Efficient movement is a matter of training the nervous system to send impulses to certain muscles, causing these muscles to contract while halting impulses to the antagonistic muscles simultaneously, allowing them to relax. Properly coordinated impulses surge with the exact intensity required to attain skill.

- We learn solely by doing. By forming proper connections in the nervous system through constant practice, the more familiar we become with the action. Greater familiarity results in a higher skill level.

5. *Flexibility*

- Is the range of possible motion in a joint or series of joints.
- Flexibility is developed through proper stretching exercises, and contributes to better athletic performance while decreasing the risk of injury, such as muscle strains and pulls.
- It is beneficial to precede flexibility exercises with endurance training.
- Flexibility has been proven to improve when there is an elevation in the internal temperature of the body, which results from endurance training.

6. *Timing*

- Is the sudden reaction to a stimulus. It includes the ability to realize the right moment for executing an action.
- Timing is best exemplified by a movement that is initiated without obvious preparation and proceeds smoothly without deliberation such that it succeeds in hitting the opponent before he is alerted and has a chance to defend.
- The exact moment of launching an offensive must be seized instinctively. For example, a blow should be made when the opponent's concentration is misdirected or when he is deceived out of position.
- Reaction time is affected immensely by one's psychological and physiological conditions. Being properly warmed up also has some influence.
- Movement time is the time taken to perform a single arm/leg technique, or foot manipulation. Such timing varies according to the speed of each trainee.
- Timing a blow is a critical ingredient of powerful hitting. A good pankratiast will attempt to beat his opponent to the attack by taking the initiative and forcing the reaction of his foe. This is best accomplished by hitting him as he moves in, is lured into moving in (drawing), or as he prepares to launch an attack.
- Speed, both physically and mentally, is the essence of timing. When applied at the opportune moment, speed, together with shrewd judgment, will ensure the success of any offensive or defensive technique.
- The initiation, or start of a technique's execution, is of primary relevance in the consideration of timing. Unlike baseball players or golfers who take practice swings to commence their particular movements, the fighter must react in an instant. A failure in timing could be disastrous.

7. *Accuracy*

- Is the quality of landing one's blows with precision on an intended target.
- Nomatter how potentially destructive one's blow or kick, it will be ineffective if it does not land on the "mark."
- Accuracy requires a familiarity with the vital points of the human anatomy (eyes, neck, solar plexus, ribs, thigh, shin, etc.).

8. Endurance

- Is the capability of the body to resist fatigue while performing a prolonged, relatively strenuous activity.
- There are two distinct types of endurance: muscular & cardiovascular.
- Muscular endurance is the quality of the muscles to remain strong and in a constant state of relaxation over extended periods of time. Cardiovascular endurance (stamina) is the quality of the heart, lungs, and circulatory system to function effectively for prolonged time intervals.
- Cardiovascular endurance training is of the aerobic-type, and involves the large musculature of the lower limbs. Running, biking, rope-jumping, bagwork for three minutes, and sparring are all excellent exercises for this purpose.

9. Agility

- Is the ability to quickly and nimbly change the direction of the movement of the body. In combat, an agile fighter is one who can continually frustrate the offensives attempted by his opponent.

10. Balance

- Refers to the control of one's center of gravity during moving, attacking, and defending. Proper balance is necessary in the execution of kicking, striking, and grappling techniques.
- Balance must be studied in motion, not from a rigid, immobile posture.
- Good balance is important for follow-up movements. Be careful of an over-commitment in penetrating attacks.

MENTAL ATTRIBUTES

1. The Killer Instinct

- We all possess the "killer instinct", that ability to survive at all costs, but at different levels. These levels exist in accordance with our personalities; the more aggressive-type will have the greater intensity to win, even it if means maiming his opponent.
- The worst enemy in combat is your own self-doubt and fear. You must conquer all negative thoughts and feelings of intimidation. You must give your all at every opportunity, and demand more of your own capabilities than you feel is possible. Once a fight commences, you cannot question your chances. The outcome often depends on your determination.

2. Awareness

- Awareness of one's surroundings in combat is essential to victory. You must attempt to out-think your rival, and gain the most advantageous positions from which to attack.

- The goal is to exploit the weaknesses of your opponent while avoiding his strengths.
- Employ those tools which work best for you. Mount a relentless onslaught once you have your foe hurt, or have him in obvious trouble.

3. *The Ability To Take It*

- Overcome the subconscious fear of getting hurt if hit. Condition the body to take shots there. Develop evasiveness to dissipate the force of blows directed to the head.

4. *The Rules of the Street*

- In modern pankration's definition of street-fighting, one rule prevails; there are NO rules!! You do anything you can to avoid being injured or maimed. It is the "KILL OR BE KILLED" attitude that prevails here. Snapping the opponent's neck, ripping out his eye, biting his ear off, etc. is all within the all-out philosophy of this martial art.
- Full-contact sparring is the best means of preparing for a street-fight, but it is only a simulation and not the exact same thing. Mu tau pankration training attempts to capture its essence, but the outcome of a sparring match is immensely different from that on the street.

Δ. MU TAU PANKRATION PRODUCTS

For the latest clothing, instructional media, and products which bear the trademarked logo of mu tau pankration, contact our official website (considered the worldwide pankration information resource) at:
http://www.channel1.com/pankration/.

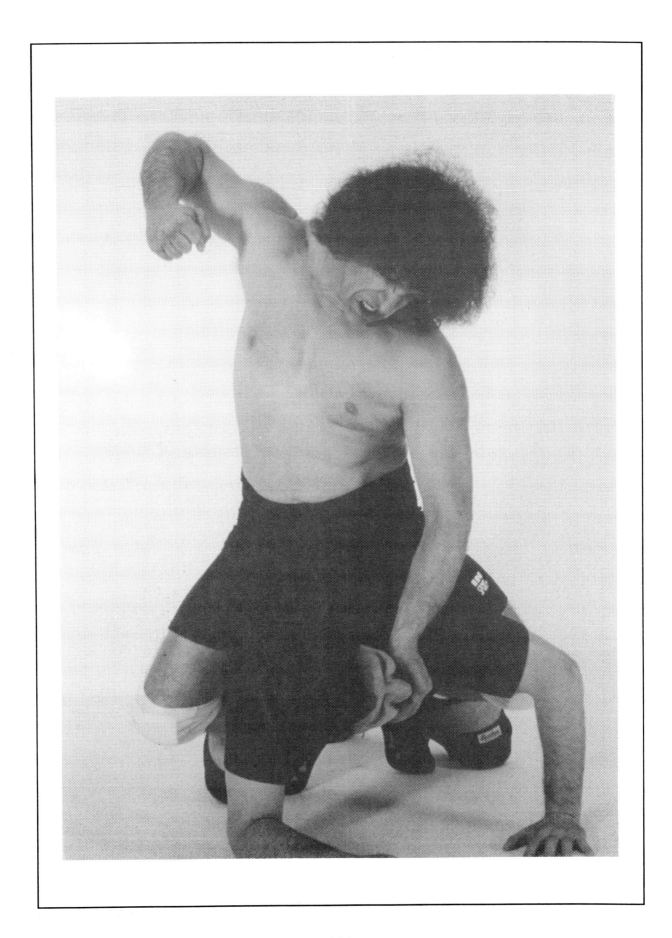

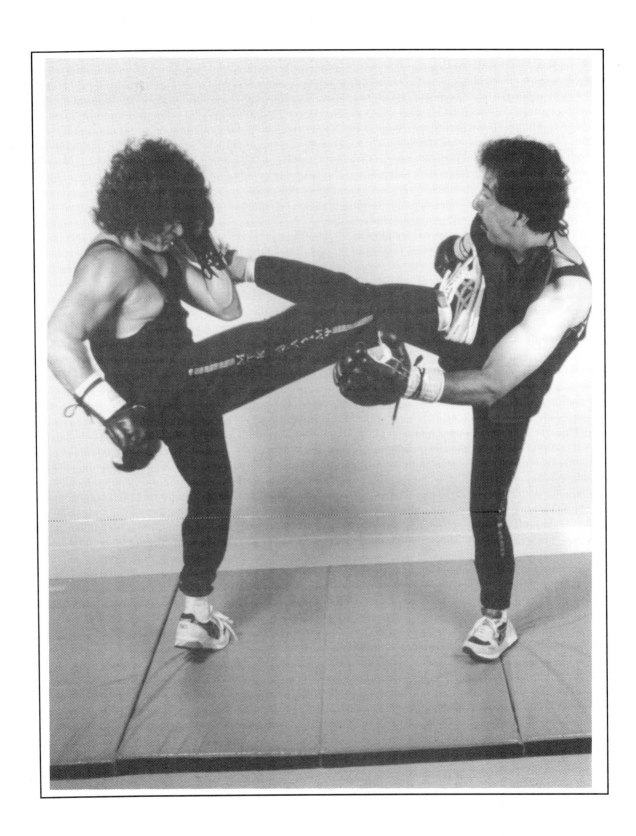